OTHER VOLUMES IN THIS SERIES

THE
BEST
AMERICAN
POETRY
1995

◇ ◇ ◇

Richard Howard, Editor

David Lehman, Series Editor

A TOUCHSTONE BOOK

PUBLISHED BY SIMON & SCHUSTER

NEW YORK • LONDON • TORONTO • SYDNEY • TOKYO • SINGAPORE

TOUCHSTONE
Rockefeller Center
1230 Avenue of the Americas
New York, NY 10020

TOUCHSTONE and colophon are registered trademarks
of Simon & Schuster Inc.

Manufactured in the United States of America

1   3   5   7   9   10   8   6   4   2

ISBN 0-684-80151-5
ISSN 1040-5763

CONTENTS

David Lehman was born in New York City in 1948. He graduated from Columbia College and attended Cambridge University in England as a Kellett Fellow. He is the author of three books of poems, including *Valentine Place*, which Scribner will publish in 1996. His prose books include *Signs of the Times: Deconstruction and the Fall of Paul de Man* and *The Perfect Murder*. *The Big Question* (1995) is the second of his critical books to appear in the University of Michigan Press's Poets on Poetry series. He is on the core faculty of the low-residency graduate writing program at Bennington College and has taught at Columbia and the New School for Social Research. In 1991 he received a three-year writer's award from the Lila Wallace–Reader's Digest Fund. He was the Elliston Poet at the University of Cincinnati in 1995. He divides his time between Ithaca, New York, and New York City.

FOREWORD

by David Lehman

◇ ◇ ◇

A recent survey of Americans indicates that many are suspicious of art. "I'm glad it exists," one woman said. "But I don't necessarily like it in my house." That may sum up a current attitude toward painting. With poetry, however, it's a different story—the opposite story. Everyone seems to be writing the stuff or talking about poetry's resurgence. The very word *poet* remains an honorific, if only when applied to singers and politicians. New York governor Mario Cuomo, on the eve of electoral defeat, struck *Newsweek*'s Joe Klein as "a public poet in Autumn." The same magazine's headline writers hailed Bruce Springsteen and Merle Haggard as "Two Poets of the Common Man." And when Kurt Cobain of the rock group Nirvana blew his brains out, the *New York Times* put the news on the front page, declaring the passing of the "Hesitant Poet of 'Grunge Rock.' " Journalism's herd of independent minds immediately picked up not only the story but the poetic spin, and the newsweeklies chimed in with obits of "The Poet of Alienation."

All through 1994 the evidence continued to mount. Either there really is a big new boom in poetry, or there has been one all along and the media have just caught on. Daily newspapers and Sunday supplements tirelessly recycle their obligatory features on the proliferation of poetry readings across America. The spoken word is in the spotlight at dank cellar bars, reminding the reporter on the beat of late-1950s visions of ecstatic transcendence, incense, bongo drums, and the meaning of life.

Allen Ginsberg in particular has quickened the ardor of the fourth estate. You can tell that the khaki-clad author of *Howl*—and of the new book *Cosmopolitan Greetings*—is back in the press's good graces by the sudden fixation on his finances. One week last September,

New York magazine reported that Ginsberg's teaching salary at Brooklyn College is just shy of six figures, and the next week the *Times* disclosed that the poet had sold his papers to Stanford University for a million dollars. Whether the conjunction of Allen Ginsberg and Mammon proves that the fates are ironists, or that capitalism and the counterculture always could coexist, or that being an English major needn't be the career disaster feared by a college student's anxious parents, who can say? Not Allen, who is cheerfully up to his old tricks: he chanted a protest poem entitled "Hum Bom" from the pitcher's mound in Candlestick Park in June. At least somebody played ball in 1994.

The success of *Dead Poets Society* a few years ago confounded Hollywood insiders, who felt that the movie's title consisted of the three least attractive words in the language. In Hollywood, one successful picture kicks off a trend, and in 1994, Dorothy Parker's poems punctuated *Mrs. Parker and the Vicious Circle*. In *Four Weddings and a Funeral*, a poem by W. H. Auden is recited at the most dour of the eponymous events, and it so moved audiences that Random House published a slender paperback with "Funeral Blues" plus nine other Auden poems in a hot-selling edition of forty thousand copies. At Jackie Kennedy's funeral, Maurice Tempelsman, her longtime companion, read C. P. Cavafy's poem "Ithaka," a wonderful choice; Cavafy's American readership tripled overnight. On Halloween, fifteen thousand copies of a book containing "The Raven" were distributed free at public libraries. They made an event of it in Austin, Texas, where someone from the coroner's office and someone from the department of taxation gave a "death-and-taxes" reading of Poe's haunting poem. "Fun," a poem by Vermont poet Wyn Cooper, became the nation's number-one rock hit, "All I Wanna Do," by Sheryl Crow, which reached the double platinum mark in sales. (When the song won the 1995 Grammy Award for Record of the Year, Crow said backstage that she had written "five different sets of lyrics for that song, and all of them sucked," before Cooper's poem saved the day.) Meanwhile, *Cats* continues on Broadway, which means that T. S. Eliot's volume of feline light verse has made more money for the Eliot estate than the rest of his writings combined.

Some would argue that all this activity obscures the point, which is that poetry is at a serious disadvantage in the culture of celebrity. The idea of lasting fame, as Milton wrote about it in "Lycidas," is as fundamental to poetry as it is anomalous in the era of the abbreviated attention span. "Fame is the spur that the clear spirit doth raise / (That last infirmity of noble mind) / To scorn delights, and live laborious days," Milton wrote. The desire for fame has always motivated poets. But the fame that Milton had in mind is not the fabrication of "broad rumour," the product of buzz and hype. It is the serene judgment of immortality:

> Fame is no plant that grows on mortal soil,
> Not in the glistering foil
> Set off to the world, nor in broad rumour lies,
> But lives and spreads aloft by those pure eyes,
> And perfect witness of all-judging Jove;
> As he pronounces lastly on each deed,
> Of so much fame in heaven expect thy meed.

Fame thus nobly conceived remains the poet's spur. But fame conceived as fifteen minutes of media attention, in which intense exposure is followed by erasure, is hospitable not to poetry but to an image or representation of it, a simulacrum.

The reading public doesn't always recognize the real thing. "We complain that it doesn't sound like the way we talk," the columnist Anna Quindlen observed, "but if it sounds like the way we talk, we complain that it doesn't rhyme." When Yusef Komunyakaa's *Neon Vernacular* won the 1994 Pulitzer Prize, Quindlen noted that the book's first printing amounted to 2,500 copies, "which is fairly large for poetry but a joke to the folks who stock those racks at the airport." It is a truism that the only time a poem can reach America's huge moviegoing audience is when it is read aloud in a movie. But this scarcely means that poetry lacks a sizable constituency of its own. It means rather that poetry stands in the same relation to literary culture that jazz and classical music stand in relation to the culture of noise. The audience is there in significant numbers, and you will not overlook it unless your frame of reference is the national TV audience for a celebrity murder trial.

The Best American Poetry depends on the vitality of the art on the one hand, and on the attentions of a receptive readership on the other. We are lucky to have both. We are lucky also to have Richard Howard as the year's guest editor. *Like Most Revelations* (1994), Mr. Howard's latest collection of poems, was short-listed for the

National Book Award; he won the 1970 Pulitzer Prize in poetry and the 1983 American Book Award in translation for his complete version of Baudelaire's *Les Fleurs du mal*. Not only is he a translator of renown but an important teacher and literary editor, who has a great history of discovering and nurturing poets, publishing them in one or another of the fine magazines he has served as poetry editor. (The list includes *New American Review*, *Shenandoah*, *The New Republic*, *The Paris Review*, and *Western Humanities Review*; he remains poetry editor of the last two named.) Editing *The Best American Poetry 1995* seemed like a natural extension of his customary exertions.

It is characteristic of Richard that early on he laid down several laws governing this year's book. No poet would be eligible who had served as a guest editor in this series. Moreover, no poet would be eligible who had appeared in three or more previous volumes. At a stroke these edicts eliminated the work of Ammons, Ashbery, Bradley, Clampitt, Creeley, Fulton, Glück, Graham, Hall, Hass, Hollander, Howard, Koch, Levine, Merrill, Merwin, Mitchell, Moss, Pinsky, Rich, Simic, St. John, Strand, Tate, and Wilbur, among others—a formidable list. But that was the point. The limitation would mean that for this particular year the aim would be, in Mr. Howard's words, "not an anthology of confirmation but an anthology of surprise, even astonishment."

The accent is on discovery. We have come up with many new poets; forty-nine have never previously appeared in *The Best American Poetry*. It says something about the depth of American poetry that such notables as Margaret Atwood, Irving Feldman, Allen Ginsberg, Heather McHugh, Grace Schulman, and David Wagoner appear this year for the first time. Poems were chosen from fifty magazines, more than ever before. The proportion of poems from little magazines (as opposed to wide-circulation periodicals such as *The New Yorker* and *The Atlantic*) went way up. There were more poems in verse forms, intricate or homemade: the book contains two villanelles, two sestinas, three sonnet-chains, and a poem in the shape of history's widening gyre. Some of the poems exemplify the idea that poets keep the conscience of society. There are poems here about Bosnia, urban violence, political injustice, French collaborationism, and gays in the military. Other poems treat the hard-boiled romance of *film noir*, the landscape of New Mexico or that of a scruffy suburban hill, fairy tales and Zen Buddhist koans,

Frank O'Hara and Miles Davis, Tarzan and *Citizen Kane*, but also language and its properties, birth, childhood, brotherhood, masturbation, sex, friendship, marriage, children, childlessness, and death.

Last winter the poet who goes by the name of Sparrow went with some downtown friends to the offices of *The New Yorker*, where they staged a sit-in to protest the poetry published in that magazine. "Personally, I think our poets are just as bad as their poets, but at least we have a sense of humor," said Sparrow. "We demand to get published in *The New Yorker*—because we're just as bad as they are." Knowing there are places where the word *bad* means its opposite, I want to assure Sparrow that our doors are open and that the best bad poems of the year stand a fighting chance of getting in. To honor "the best" in any field is perhaps a daring thing to do at a time when many cultural institutions are full of doubt and self-doubt. But it is a dare one may confidently take up. Modern American poetry is a cultural glory on the level of jazz and abstract expressionism. It is constantly renewing and refreshing itself, and so the spirit of discovery will always play as great a part in the making of this anthology as the pleasures of abundance.

Richard Howard was born in Cleveland, Ohio, in 1929. He was educated at Columbia University and the Sorbonne. He has published ten books of poetry; for his third, *Untitled Subjects*, he received the Pulitzer Prize in 1970. A distinguished translator of French literature, he has received the P.E.N. Translation Medal, the Ordre National Mérite from the French government, and the American Book Award for his translation of Baudelaire's *Les Fleurs du mal*. He has translated more than 150 works from the French. His comprehensive critical study, *Alone with America: Essays on the Art of Poetry in the United States* (1970), was reissued in an enlarged edition in 1980. He is a member of the American Academy and Institute of Arts and Letters and a chancellor of the Academy of American Poets, and in 1994–95 he served as the Poet Laureate of New York State. He is poetry editor of both *The Paris Review* and *Western Humanities Review*. He is University Professor of English at the University of Houston.

INTRODUCTION

by Richard Howard

◇   ◇   ◇

Who now?
SAMUEL BECKETT

Crisp and creditable emerge (not messily protrude) from the hands that gathered them the initial seven volumes in this series—not gathered *poems*, we are from the first reminded by the annual title, but that grander undeterminable thing *poetry*. As the bright compilations queue up on the shelf, what pleasure, what exaltations they afford that curiosity of ours so often (and so erroneously) called idle! And yet no sooner is it assuaged than our querying interest, unpropped by ideology, unstayed by partisanship, discovers that in the course of the accumulating heptad, and increasingly! our pleasure and even our exaltations are notably those of recognition, even of confirmation.

Elbowing out (or is it some other body-English here: stiff-arming, even bellying-up?) the unfamiliar, the downright strange, American Poetry at its "Best" appears determined to demonstrate Darwin at his most theoretically brutal; the grand old names inveterately appear, the long-since-agreed-upon Best American Poets, and the names of the former editors, too, indispensably answer that optimal role call, ever more numerous and always more distinguished, certainly, than the merely new, the more or less surprising, so unfit or at least so unfitted into our notion of what is to be warranted as "Best Poetry." Apparently we cannot, if we are to have the best poetry, year by year, do without them; and yet with them, those predictable blue chips and gilt edges, is there, by now, much room remaining for whatever is epactal, extra, *else*?

When Mr. Lehman asked me to join him in the selection of the poems for the eighth book in the series, I was of course delighted to take my place in the uniformly select line-up of selectors—who would not, after all, revel in being regarded as yet another one of *them*? But might we not, I asked him, even without changing the ominous title which echoed, to my ears, so forbiddingly (as if someone had to be reassured that *that* was what the stuff was, "poetry" all right)—might we not, by a little editorial stipulation and topiary, arrange matters differently, so that the annual product, for once (my successor could always change back to the good old ways, the dear departed attainment of what in seven years had become anthological orthodoxy), would yield (*sic*) the gratification of surprise rather than of recognition, the delights of—even—confusion rather than of confirmation? Baudelaire, who coined the Tradition of the New, once said that if the greatest of all pleasures is to be surprised, the only other pleasure nearly so great is to *give* surprise. Perhaps both can be managed here?

The series editor said we might.

Therefore poets whose work has appeared three or more times in this series are here and now ineligible, as are all seven former editors of the series. Their absence may be noted as a badge of distinction, a virtual presence—what Miss Dickinson calls "the missing all." Whereupon the seventy-five poems anthologized this time afford, it seems to me, rather a different accounting of the year's yield (that word again!), though some noted, even some notorious poets do appear in the series for the first time with this issue. The difference is to be experienced, I daresay, in the reading, not in any greedy generalization which might be offered by way of an introduction. Indeed a chief commonality I can observe is the appeal (to my own taste) for a poetry of homage: there is quite a representation, here, of poems credited and debted to other (especially anterior) poets and artists, though I grant that such reflexivity may be more the consequence of my preference than any specific manifestation of the Muse in 1994.

Another characteristic of this year's choices is the likelihood of the long poem. Not so very long, as I have had occasion to remark in another place; not long the way Merrill or Ammons or Ashbery have been so opulently long. But longish; not the lyric instance, the discursive turn, the dramatic swipe, but something so commodious as to require a spine or at least cartilaginous tissue, call it a protocol. Such poems, as represented here, have devised methods of holding on, or up, or out—every adverbial preposition but *back* (and even in this direction, one finds that restraint, too, can be one of the weapons in the armory of the extended poem). In all, what is to be noted is a certain extravagance in the utterance which is clearly and plainly delighted to be thus enabled to carry itself out, voices euphoric at their capacity to be not only raised but made resident in the reader's mind until the proper occasion for release. Energy, we realize, is our immediate stipulation, and the rest, as James's odd hero says—the rest is the madness of art.

In our magazine culture, the extended poem is a gauge of morale: printed and read by those who enjoy poetry, a hardy band of bardy hands, rather than only—only!—acknowledged *in passing* by those who regard poetry as a good thing to have around in sparing doses (say, at the bottom of prose columns), though rather a trial *in the long run*. It is worth remarking, then, that on all sides—and sides there are, in the Tong wars of our poetry—burgeons a certain periodical willingness to run (or certainly to run down) the risks, since "long" always forebodes *longueurs*. In the longish poems reprinted here, I believe such specters (impatience with any expression longer than the MTV episode) have been forestalled by the prompt delivery *throughout* of news, truth, invention, even beauty: accomplished claims upon our much beleaguered attention, our interest, our hopes.

Elsewhere and in the wonderfully varied short run, I believe the poems evidence (judicious as well as judiciary term) an ulterior prevalence of utterance, of *vocalise* over extended argument, over the long-term understanding. American poetry these days strikes me as very much *for the nonce*, a provisional stating of the case. Since our poetry (best or not: a culture is no better than its verse) is the myth by which we live and love and have our seeing, such temporizing is not unfamiliar, even if the poems are. Contemporary myth, Roland Barthes has observed, is discontinuous. It is no longer stated in extended, constituted narratives, but only in "discourse." It is phraseology.

Here then are a lot of poems by which (in which) seventy-five poets, those representative beings, phrased our existence in 1994, a year in which many other things were done and undone. I am sometimes shocked by them, shaken certainly, even, once or twice, shamed; chiefly, I think, I am shown what it is like to be alive. Were we to be asked, as by some exalted tribunal from our own religious history or by some extraterrestrial inquiry, what our life on earth had to say for itself, the ensuing volume is, I believe, a fair response—fair and rising. Such an inquiry, such a tribunal is, of course, always and only a projection of our own hopes and fears ("this thing of darkness I acknowledge mine"), as I readily concede in the case of what my repudiation of competition in poetry identifies, nonetheless, as the Best Poetry for 1995, or the way we live now.

THE
BEST
AMERICAN
POETRY
1995

◇ ◇ ◇

Bored

◊ ◊ ◊

All those times I was bored
out of my mind. Holding the log
while he sawed it. Holding
the string while he measured, boards,
distances between things, or pounded
stakes into the ground for rows and rows
of lettuces and beets, which I then (bored)
weeded. Or sat in the back
of the car, or sat still in boats,
sat, sat, while at the prow, stern, wheel
he drove, steered, paddled. It
wasn't even boredom, it was looking,
looking hard and up close at the small
details. Myopia. The worn gunwales,
the intricate twill of the seat
cover. The acid crumbs of loam, the granular
pink rock, its igneous veins, the sea-fans
of dry moss, the blackish and then the greying
bristles on the back of his neck.
Sometimes he would whistle, sometimes
I would. The boring rhythm of doing
things over and over, carrying
the wood, drying
the dishes. Such minutiae. It's what
the animals spend most of their time at,
ferrying the sand, grain by grain, from their tunnels,
shuffling the leaves in their burrows. He pointed
such things out, and I would look
at the whorled texture of his square finger, earth under

the nail. Why do I remember it as sunnier
all the time then, although it more often
rained, and more birdsong?
I could hardly wait to get
the hell out of there to
anywhere else. Perhaps though
boredom is happier. It is for dogs or
groundhogs. Now I wouldn't be bored.
Now I would know too much.
Now I would know.

from *The Atlantic Monthly*

Nocturnal

◇ ◇ ◇

Their bedroom window's open one flight up—
I used to panic when boys walked me
to the porch, what might they hear?
Now, we come outside for Mike to smoke
and I wonder how deep asleep they are,
if they can smell it, if our quiet evening voices
offer just a murmur or a cause to strain
and try to hear.

We imagine our new house,
or rented rooms, how many rooms?
By the river or closer to the town
that only one of us so far has seen?
In June we'll take a trip to look together.
For now, indulgence, fantasy: a tub with feet,
claws curved against white tiles, a window wide
and low—long view.

We lapse into impossible desires—other states,
whole farms with horses, plots of vegetables.
We laugh too loud and hear a cough—polite,
requesting, and then my mother laughs herself.
Come on, I call, *come out!* The sash creaks farther up,
and down around the roof my father's voice:
he hasn't been awake this late in years,
nor had a cigarette, has got to work tomorrow.
My mother joins him at the screen and says,
Look—half a moon.

We four all listen to each other
though there's nothing much to hear. I am imagining
the way they look, my mom's blue nightgown
loose and falling toward the sill, my father
in his p.j.'s kneeling so his face can reach the air.
It's an easy blessing to inhabit, facing all
the darkened windows down the street,
each one of us a different calm, remembering
a different time that holds us here inside the presence
we are making, our partners close at hand and then the other pair
we cannot see.

from *Southwest Review*

Mr. X

◇   ◇   ◇

                                 All my Ex's
live in Texas, so the country song says and no excuses,
it's mostly true for me too that the spade-shaped extra
big state with its cotton lints and Ruby Reds holds the crux
of my semi-truck-I've-never-had-any-kind-of-luck-deluxe-
super-high-jinx-born-to-be-unhappy-if-it-ain't-broken-don't-fix-

it loves, for example, there was the snakebit mudlogger who fixed
himself forever diving off that hexed bridge, and that foxy ex-
patriot who imported exotic parrots, he'd pump me up with his
        deluxe
stuff, the salesman who felt so guilty for the wide-eyed excuses
he told his wife that at the Big Six Motel just outside Las Cruces
he spent the afternoon hunched over Exodus, bemoaning the sin of
        extra-

marital sex, and the harmonica player, his mouth organ could extract
an oily bended blues, on sticky nights we'd hit the 12th hole pond
        with a fix
of Dos Equis and a hit of Ecstasy and I'd wrap my legs around his
        lanky crux,
as moonlight cut through the water like a giant X-ray, his Hohner ax
glistened in and out. And then there was the feckless shrink. No
        excuse
for his fixation, the tax man, the cute butcher from the Deluxe,

the Kilim dealer, the defrocked priest. So what if my mother was deluxe
luscious, my father with a Baptist streak, I can't blame them, I was born just extra
affectionate. Don't ask about the abortions, and who can ever make excuses
for the time I spent holed up with the Port-O-Can tycoon my friend fixed
me up with, or the Mexican sculptor who made cathedral-sized onyx X's,
twisted crucifixes. Art, he quoted Marx, was history at its crux.

Then there was the Ph.D. who took me to Peru and showed me Crux
(the Southern Cross), Centaurus, Musca, Vela, Lupus, and another deluxe
equatorial constellation that I forgot. For fun I ascribed each sparkly X
a name and date, so now I have a star chart to exalt each of my extra-
ordinary, heavenly bodies. But that night I dreamed the stars were fixed
on stacks of pages: pica asterisks to indicate omission, footnotes, excuses,

explanations. I stood there, Ms. D. Giovanni, with a million excuses.
Now in exile I journey on the Styx with Mr. X in our boat the *Crux
Criticorum*. I wear an aqua slicker, he a sharkskin suit. He's non-fiction,
never incognito. We've got our sextant and spy manual open on our deluxe
waterbed. I can just make out the tattoo above his boxers in this extra
dark, there's the curve of his back. Now we'll break the code and go beyond X.

from *Chelsea*

Schadenfreude

◇ ◇ ◇

If this were a movie, the sound of sizzling would foretell disaster
because you're walking out of the room leaving something cooking
because you have too many burners going
There should be the sound of trumpets, thin and mournful
You're going to walk into your murder.
It begins to smoke.
All the same I'm humming.
The attacker hides behind the door.
I'm whistling a happy face.
Minutes before you start shrieking, again and again
before the plaster falls down around you
before the strangulation begins
folding up clothes and putting them into drawers—your back
turned—
while the skillet, in close-up, keeps sizzling.
Minutes before the shrieking and choking.
The cupboards become lit.
Watch the doll's mouth melt.
This audience won't pity you
like big round workers who don't get pity
when they step on bus steps in the morning and make the bus
sag momentarily. Like wizened-up bodies
holding canes, heads bowed under golf hats
on their ways downtown—
This audience will laugh—
the way your eyes bulge out and your tongue is unhinged
how you return to find a kitchen filled with smoke
when we all know it's your gluttony that's caused it.
(It's the way you locked your lies up in the closet

that's led me to hate you.)
So when your doom comes—
a knife thuds into your back, let's say,
or an arrow is shot into your ribs
or a razor is pulled across your face
or you trip on a roller skate near the open cellar stairs
or you walk into a sliding glass door
or you are hung from the shower curtain rod in a plastic white shower
or you are stabbed with pinking shears
or demoralized with an axe handle
or beaten down the spine with a rake
or forced to swallow some golf balls
or sliced at the waist and the wounds salted
or if you merely carpet-burned your arm on the carpet
It will feel great to watch
you get it
or at least to see you experience
some slight, future discomfort,
chagrin,
embarrassment.

from *American Poetry Review*

Sunday, Tarzan in His Hammock

◇ ◇ ◇

When the king of the jungle first wakes up, he thinks
it's going to be a great day, as laden with possibility
as the banana tree with banana hands, but by ten
he's still in the hammock, arms and legs dull as
termite mounds. He stares at the thatched roof and realizes
that his early good mood was a leftover from Saturday,
when he got so much done: a great day, he saved
the tiger cub trapped in the banyan, herded the hippos
away from the tourists and their cameras and guns,
restrung and greased the N-NW vines, and all by noon.
All day he went about his duties, not so much kingly duties
as custodial, and last night, he and Cheetah went for a walk
under the ostrich-egg moon. This morning nothing stirs him.
The world is a stagnant river, a scummy creek's dammed pool.
Cheetah's gone chattering off, Jane is in town,
and the rest of the animals are busy with one another—
fighting, eating, mating. Tarzan can barely move,
he does not want to move. Does the gazelle ever feel this
lassitude, does it ever want to lie down and just stare,
no longer caring for its own safety, tired of the vigilance?
Does the lion, fat in the grass, ever think, fuck it,
let the wounded springbok live, who cares?
Tarzan thinks maybe he'll go to the bathing pools
and watch the village girls bathe, splashing in the sun,
their breasts and thighs perfect. He wishes someone
would bring him a gourd of palm wine, a platter

of imported fruits—kiwi, jack fruit, star fruit—
or maybe a bowl of roasted yams slathered in goat butter.
Maybe Jane will bring him a book.
He hears far off in the dense canopy a zebra's cry for help,
those damned jackals again, but, no, he will not move.
Let the world take care of itself, let the world eat
the world. He can live without the call of the wild.
He thinks.

from *ZYZZYVA*

The Woman Who Loved Things

◇　◇　◇

A woman finally learned how to love things, so things learned
how to love her too as she pressed herself to their shining sides,
their porous surfaces. She smoothed along walls until walls
smoothed along her too, a joy, a climax, this flesh
against plaster, the sweet suck of consenting molecules.

Sensitive men and women became followers, wrapping themselves
in violet, pasting her image over their fast hearts,
pressing against walls until walls came to appreciate
differences in molecules. This became a worship.
They became a love. A church. A cult. A way of being.

But, of course, it had to be: the woman's love kept growing
until she was loved by trees and appliances, from toasters
to natural obstacles, until her ceiling shook loose to send kisses,
sheets wound tight betwixt her legs, and floorboards broke free
of their nails, straining their lengths over her sleeping.

She awoke and drove out of town alone. In love, rocks flew
through her car windows, then whole hillsides slid, loosening
with desire. Her car shattered its shaft to embrace her,
but she ran from the wreckage, calling all the sweet things
as she waited in a field of strangely complacent daisies.

She spoke of love until losing her breath, and the things
trilled to feel that loss too, at last, sighing in thingness.
She fell down, and the things fell down around her. She cried,
"Christ!" and the things cried "Christ!" in their thing-hearts
until everything living and unliving wonderfully collided.

from *Harvard Review*

RAFAEL CAMPO

The Battle Hymn
of the Republic

◊ ◊ ◊

Defending you, my country, hurts
My eyes. I see the drums, the glory,
The marching through the gory,
Unthinkable mud of soldiers' guts

And opened hearts: I want to serve.
I join the military,
Somehow knowing that I'll never marry.
The barracks' silence as I shave

Is secretive and full of cocks.
I think to myself, *What if I'm a queer,*
What if too many years
Go by and then my brain unlocks—

The days seem uniformed,
Crisp salutes in all the trees;
A sandstorm buries the casualties
Of a war. *What if I were born*

This way, I think to myself,
What if I were dead,
An enemy bullet in my head.
I see the oil burning in the Gulf,

Which hurts my eyes. My sergeant cries.
Now he's a real man—
I sucked his cock behind a van
In the Presidio, beneath a sky

So full of orange clouds
I thought I was in love.
I think to myself, *What have
I become?* I lose myself in the crowds

Of the Castro, the months go by
And suddenly they want to lift the ban.
I don't think they can.
I still want to die

My death of honor, I want to die
Defending values I don't understand;
The men I see walking hand in hand
Bring this love song to my mind.

from *Ploughshares*

Girl Writing a Letter

◇ ◇ ◇

A thief drives to the museum in his black van. The night
watchman says Sorry, closed, you have to come back tomorrow.
The thief sticks the point of his knife in the guard's ear.
I haven't got all evening, he says, I need some art.
Art is for pleasure, the guard says, not possession, you can't
something, and then the duct tape is going across his mouth.
Don't worry, the thief says, we're both on the same side.
He finds the Dutch Masters and goes right for a Vermeer:
"Girl Writing a Letter." The thief knows what he's doing.
He has a Ph.D. He slices the canvas on one edge from
the shelf holding the salad bowls right down to the
square of sunlight on the black and white checked floor.
The girl doesn't hear this, she's too absorbed in writing
her letter, she doesn't notice him until too late. He's
in the picture. He's already seated at the harpsichord.
He's playing the G Minor Sonata by Domenico Scarlatti,
which once made her heart beat till it passed the harpsichord
and raced ahead and waited for the music to catch up.
She's worked on this letter for three hundred and twenty years.
Now a man's here, and though he's dressed in some weird clothes,
he's playing the harpsichord for her, for her alone, there's no one
else alive in the museum. The man she was writing to is dead—
time to stop thinking about him—the artist who painted her is dead.
She should be dead herself, only she has an ear for music
and a heart that's running up the staircase of the Gardner Museum
with a man she's only known for a few minutes, but it's
true, it feels like her whole life. So when the thief
hands her the knife and says *you* slice the paintings out
of their frames, you roll them up, she does it; when he says

you put another strip of duct tape over the guard's mouth
so he'll stop talking about aesthetics, she tapes him, and when
the thief puts her behind the wheel and says, drive, baby,
the night is ours, it is the Girl Writing a Letter who steers
the black van on to the westbound ramp for Storrow Drive
and then to the Mass Pike, it's the Girl Writing a Letter who
drives eighty miles an hour headed west into a country
that's not even discovered yet, with a known criminal, a van
full of old masters and nowhere to go but down, but for the
Girl Writing a Letter these things don't matter, she's got a beer
in her free hand, she's on the road, she's real and she's in love.

from *The Iowa Review*

Terminus

◇　◇　◇

Here is a piece of required reading
at the end of our century
the end of a millennium that began with the Crusades

The transcript of an interview
between a Red Cross doctor
and a Muslim girl in Bosnia
twelve years old
who described her rape by men
calling themselves soldiers
different men every night one after the other
six seven eight of them
for a week
while she was chained by the neck
to a bed in her former schoolhouse
where she saw her parents and her brothers
have their throats slit and tongues cut out
where her sister-in-law
nineteen years old and nursing her baby
was also raped night after night
until she dared to beg for water
because her milk had run dry
at which point one of the men
tore the child from her arms
and as if he were "cutting an ear of corn"
(the girl's words)
lopped off the child's head
with a hunting knife
tossed it into the mother's lap

and raped the girl again
slapping her face
smearing it with her nephew's blood
and then shot the mother
who had begun to shriek
with the head wide-eyed in her lap
shoving his gun into her mouth
and firing twice

All of this recounted to the doctor
in a monotone
a near whisper in a tent
beside an icy river
where the girl had turned up frostbitten
wearing only a soiled slip
her hair yanked out
her teeth broken

All the history you've ever read
tells you this is what men do
this is only a sliver of the reflection
of the beast
who is a fixture of human history
and the places you heard of as a boy
that were his latest stalking grounds
Auschwitz Dachau Treblinka
and the names of their dead
and their numberless dead whose names have vanished
each day now find their rolls swelled
with kindred souls
new names new numbers
from towns and villages
that have been scorched from the map

1993 may as well be 1943
and it should be clear now
that the beast in his many guises
the flags and vestments

in which he wraps himself
and the elaborate titles he assumes
can never be outrun

As that girl with the broken teeth
loaded into an ambulance
strapped down on a stretcher
so she wouldn't claw her own face
will never outrun him
no matter where she goes
solitary or lost in a crowd
the line she follows
however straight or crooked
will always lead her back to that room
like the chamber at the bottom
of Hell in the Koran
where the Zaqqūm tree grows
watered by scalding rains
"bearing fruit like devils' heads"

In not giving her name
someone has noted at the end
of the transcript that the girl herself
could not or would not recall it
and then describes her as a survivor

Which of course is from the Latin
meaning to live on
to outlive others

I would not have used that word

from *The Paris Review*

The Infusion Room

⬦ ⬦ ⬦

1

Mercy on Maryanne who through a hole beneath her collarbone
     drinks the life-preserving fluid, while in her arm
another IV tube drips something green. "It never affects me," she
     says, "I'm fortunate."
She has Crohn's and rheumatoid arthritis and now osteoporosis, as
     well as no gamma globulin
as we all have no gamma globulin, or at least not enough. Mercy
     on Aaron,
her son, who at fifteen has Hodgkin's and arthritis and no gamma
     globulin, who is out of school
just for the moment. "He's so bright," the doctor says, "he'll make
     it up." But of course
you never (as I remember) quite make it up. (Sitting up all night so
     as not to cough,
coughing so hard I tore the cartilage off three ribs. "If I was God,"
     the then-doctor said,
"I'd design better ribs.")

Mercy on Mitzi who shook for three hours the first day I was there,
     and Cynthia
who cried because of the pain in her legs but aspires to horseback
     riding.
"Mitzi's tough," the nurse said admiringly, and I thought, could I
     ever be so tough?
Could I wear a velvet cap like Cynthia? Mitzi's on chemo.

And mercy on Paul, who drives a cab part-time and has sores on his
        ankles.
"If you could put your feet up more," the doctor suggests. He
        winces as she touches his skin, explains
if he could just finish college he could get a better job, but to finish
        college he has to drive this cab,
and I think of my luck all those years teaching at a college, the
        flexible hours, pleasant rooms
where you could always put your feet up if need be. Mercy on Mike,
the pilot, who looks like a jockey, who shows us pictures of his
        14-month-old girl,
who used to be allergic, as I am allergic, so that now while Mike
        reads the comics,
his friend leans against the wall, thumbing a computer manual,
        faithful, a tad overweight.
Mercy on the wholesale grocer, the man who sells prostheses, the
        used-Caddy salesman moving to glossy Florida,
the one who says candidly, "The first two days of each week are
        OK, then I begin to get tired."

Mercy on the black kid strapped to his Walkman, mercy on all like
        him who fall asleep.
Mercy on Sally Jessy Raphael and the interminable talk show
        flickering down the morning as we drift, or shiver, or sleep.
Aaron puts his huge sneakers up on Maryanne's seat and she holds
        his hand lightly while he sleeps;
they look like the Creation of Adam.

2

I think if you could see us now we'd resemble giant grasshoppers
whose skinny elbows vibrate slightly above their heads, or I think
        that the room

if you approached it by space ship would look like a busy harbor,
crammed with barges, their curious cargo, and cranes extended or
        at half mast,

but all functional, needed. The TV twitters. The nurses are taking
    a break
from the hard business of giving us each day (at two- or three- or
    four-week intervals)

our daily, habitable lives. We too could go on a talk show,
challenging truckers' wives, twins who have lost their Other. I peel
    open my sandwich

with my good, unencumbered right hand. The IV poles gleam, we
    float on our black recliners.
It is almost time for the soaps.

from *American Poetry Review*

Sestina

◊ ◊ ◊

He wanted to tell her the weekend idea was 'neat,'
But he kept hearing himself repeat the word 'funny.'
She named the names of trees, flowers: *sycamore, tulip.*
He asked her who did she think she was, Gary Snyder?
Above the car, then over the hotel, the spring moon
Was full, orange. 'This isn't just another fling,'

She said suddenly. 'Don't dare think it's some fling.'
The Jack Daniel's arrived, hers on the rocks, his neat.
'I didn't think that at all.' Behind her, the moon
Looked away. She fretted. 'I just—I feel funny.'
Amazingly, it occurred to him something Gary Snyder
Once said was appropriate. He repeated it. 'Tulips,'

She smiled back. 'Let's take a walk through the tulips.'
Later, they didn't make love. She was shy. Some fling,
He brooded. Did she really think he *liked* Gary Snyder—
That he, too, thought he had it all summed up in a neat
Little package? Funny, he groaned. Worse than funny.
I get it all right for once: drinks, room, even the moon

Cooperates. How often can you count on a spring moon
Slipping through the sycamores, picking out the tulips
In the night air? She should feel romantic, not 'funny'!
Lying next to her, he felt so restless, eager to fling
His body atop hers—seeking, yet in control, his need
Ascetic, sensual, yet poised—a suburban Gary Snyder . . . .

In the dark, she teased: 'Thinking about Gary Snyder?'
Then: 'I'm not so shy now.' He thought about the moon,
And a Grace Paley character who 'liked his pussy neat.'
Then she was touching him, needing him, her two lips
Soft flowers, emissaries of her body, softly ruffling
Against him, moving him, so powerfully it wasn't funny . . .

Afterward, they were awkward, shy, trying to be funny.
They couldn't get any more mileage out of Gary Snyder.
'Some fling,' he said, and she flung back, 'Some fling!'
But mostly they were quiet. Outside, the big yellow moon
Yawned. He made a mental note to send her some tulips.
She stared out the window, thinking about the word 'neat.'

★

He thought of how she'd fling her hair. And the moon . . .
It was *finito*. Next week he got a book by Gary Snyder
In the mail. That was funny. He sent her the tulips.

from *The Paris Review*

Thirty Years Rising

◇   ◇   ◇

I needed to point to the buildings, as if they all stood
for something, as if Detroit could rise again
into its own skyline, filled in
as it always is inside me:
each cracked sidewalk, each
of the uniformed girls, braided
and quiet as weeds, each bicycled boy, each man
with a car and a wife, the ones that I slept with
and arranged, neatly, like a newly laid
subdivision.

But I was driving with my brother
who doesn't like to think
of the thirty years rising
inside us, the leavened truth. He's arrived
at the heavy black X of destination
on the inside of his forehead
and he doesn't want to see me
looking like this: open-palmed
and childishly dressed, with hipbones
instead of children, aching
to put my sneakered feet on his new leather dash.

He doesn't want to hear me
say something fucked-up, something like:
It's in my bones. My sternum
runs like Woodward Avenue,
it's pinnated, parked on, full
of dirt, holding women in wigs and cigarettes, bars

lit from the outside in, it's overflowing
with pool tables and ashtrays. My ribs
are holding up factories and breweries, two-bedroom
houses and multi-storied lives, this strip,
this city, these sidestreets,
a bony feather.

He's lived here all his life.
But I gave up these streets
for so many others. I hopped
turnstiles to ride the Metro,
memorized El tracks and Muni stations
until I had a huge worn subway
map in my head, but couldn't get off at any stop,
couldn't begin to live in any city, and couldn't sleep
with anybody but myself. I gave up
this body for so many others. I've been both
an exaggeration of myself and someone
who looks just like me but sounds different.
But now I'm back
to visit both, and I need to point
to my first hotel room;
to the mortuary above which
my tall half-Chinese half-German
punkrockboyfriend fingered me
like a book in his little bed;
and to the hospital where our bonemother
died so late or so early that
we were both sound asleep.

I didn't say it,
but: My sternum is breaking
with this, it's sinking
like Woodward as Detroit rises around
my brother's turn, rises and falls.

Falls not at all like this light summer rain
but hard, like someone else's memory,
insistent, unwanted, but suddenly,
and again, being claimed.

from *Michigan Quarterly Review*

Film Noir: Train Trip Out of Metropolis

◇ ◇ ◇

We're headed for empty-headedness,
the featureless amnesias of Idaho, Montana, Nevada,
states rich only in vowel sounds and alliteration.
We're taking the train so we can see into the heart
of the heart of America framed in the windows' cool
oblongs of light. We want cottages, farmhouses
with peaked roofs leashed by wood smoke to the clouds;
we want the golden broth of sunlight ladled over
ponds and meadows. We've never seen a meadow.
Now, we want to wade into one—up to our chins in the grassy
welter—the long reach of our vision grabbing up great
handfuls and armloads of scenery, our eyes at the clouds'
white sale, our eyes at the bargain basement giveaway
of clods and scat and cow pies. We want to feel half
of America to the left of us and half to the right, ourselves
like a spine dividing the book in two, ourselves holding
the whole great story together.

And then, suddenly, the train pulls into the station,
and the scenery begins to creep forward—a friendly but timid tribe.
The ramshackle shapes of Main, the old-fashioned cars dozing
at the ribbon of curb, the mongrel hound loping across a stretch
of unpaved road, the medals of the Lions and Chamber of Commerce
pinned on the town's chest, the street lights on their long stems,
the little park, the trolley, the faint bric-a-brac of park stuff:
bum on the bench, boy with the ball come closer and closer.

Then the pleasantly sinister swell of the soundtrack tapers
to a long wail. The noise of a train gathers momentum
and disappears into the distance leaving us stranded here,
and our names are strolling across the landscape in the crisply
voluminous script of the opening credits, as though these were
our signatures on the contract, as though we were the authors of
        this story.

        from *The Antioch Review*

Sometimes I Get Distracted

◇ ◇ ◇

for Philip Whalen

Throwing a ball

like a bridge
over an old wound

like a cape
thrown chivalrously
over incoherent muck.

Catching it
is easy.

"Now toss it back,"

says the Zen monk
standing in his garden
centuries away.

from *New American Writing*

Terminal Laughs

◊ ◊ ◊

Thirty years ago the young Corso in his cups
—*my* cups, in fact, my booze, too, on which, a gulp
away from getting smashed, he was loading up.
First, tagging along, he'd crashed the party,
then was everywhere making his presence felt,
depositing impartially—on rug, on couch,
on the proffered hand and the affable lap—
steaming little signatures of self.
Introduced to me, his next-to-unknown
and near-anonymous host, Gregory exclaimed,
" 'Irving Feldman?' 'Irving *Feldman*?' 'Oiving Feldman?'
—what kind of name is that for a poet?"
He probably intended well: you know
—Touring Star Instructs Benighted Yokel In
the finer perks of fame, its *droit de seigneur:*
since one never knows who'll get the last laugh,
Maestro will make sure he grabs the first sneer.
Caught redhanded being *myself*, naked in quotes,
I contemplated the awfulness of my name
—undistinguished, uneuphonious, a joke.
What vocal apparatus would not collapse in
a fatal fibrillation of runaway yuks,
intoning those syllables with suitable awe?
Well, then, spare the world apocalypse by laughter
—just shut up, Irving, shut down, back off!
Oh, but now " 'Gregorio Nunzio Corso!' "
he tarantara-ed, nose loftily rising to
this high occasion, as if summoned upward by
the fanfaronade of its fantastic fanfare,

"now *that*, Oiving, is a name for a poet!"
Second paeon, dactyl, dactyl catalectic
—his name itself, alone, had heft and breath
enough to launch and swell a mighty fine line.
No way to know *this* poet from his poem!
—who, an hour later, crossed one line too many.
Ralph (redfaced, Anglophile), taking his measure,
tapped out deeDUM, the old iambic one-TWO,
and did a number on Gregory's nose.

It took a day or so, but finally,
gestating the guy's manners, mien, mug
while licking at my wounds, my "staircase wit,"
laggard though it was and lost in transit usually,
gagged up a furball part blood, mostly spit:
"As the poet said, Gregory, What is *in*
a name? By any other you'd be as Coarso."
The party, fortunately, had long been over,
and, bolstered by two tenderhearted ladies
covering his flanks as he retreated, while
his nose autographed in red a borrowed hanky,
the poet, faring forward, had stumbled downstairs
—to pipe his old tune in pastures not greener,
perhaps, but, for sure, far far grassier.

Skip thirty years. An eye's blink. The interim?
Some books. Some other books. Fade swiftly to:
Another party now (my son's). Another coast.
Same hubbub. Each newcomer turns the volume up.
Whom the gods would mock they first make famous.
Enter Thad. Young actor here in Hollywood,
dying for parts, money, acclaim, the glamour and
groveling and intoxication due to fame,
to be something more, but not necessarily
much more, than "just another pretty face."
He spots me there, singled out from the crowd
by the sudden celebrity that follows me
around, or maybe is leading me on:
this year's MacLaurels penciled in on my brow.
"Hey, Irving Feldman," he shouts across the tumult

of everyone madly talking all at once,
"you are a goddamn star of poetry!"
Has he ever read a word I wrote?
Still, I glow for a moment in his glee.
But somewhere behind my back I sort of hear
how Gregory, our Chatterton, our wingéd boy,
sloshed out of his cups now and into his saucer,
stubblebearded, his underwear stained with pee,
his nose no straighter for being out of joints
though longer perhaps by a thousand lines,
half toothless, and slowed to a sub-pubcrawl
—just the type, immortality's mortal bouncer,
to i.d. the gaggle at Parnassus Gate,—
I seem to hear how, guarding the lowest stair,
he mutters in his despondency (*his*, truly,
having kept his lost promise all these years),
" 'Irving Feldman,' huh? Just another pretty name."

from *The Yale Review*

DONALD FINKEL

In the Clearing

◇　◇　◇

1.

Independence Day (while for us the bugle sounds retreat).
Down in the schoolyard the fathers are offloading rockets
whereas off to the left a piledriver hasn't quit yet,
an implacable *whap whap* of the hammer, a drumfire of progress.
At the tip of each quivering dendrite dance ten thousand angels
brandishing rapiers or strumming molecular harps.

Here in the clearing, hemmed in by honeysuckle,
beleaguered by insults and promises, tocsins and prophecies,
switchblades and pheromones swarming at every pore—
it's keep treading, private, to pause is to drown.
Surrounded by windflower, speedwell, sweet yellow clover,
we can let the angels enter one at a time.

*

Few weeds are tolerant of shade. It was man who opened the sunny spots
where weeds are happiest.

How good to be back at headquarters, back at the threshold
between the labyrinth and the wilderness, one chaos and
　　　　another,
where mornings are sunny, evenings pensive, nights
　　　　incontestable.
How grand to greet the neighbors again by name,
on speaking terms with ragweed and sow-thistle,
skullcap, burdock, bitterroot and nettle,

intimate, familiar, thick as thieves.
Time was, I made way for my cohorts,
slashing and burning from here to the capital
without respite, without reflection.
How sweet to be home again with my people,
a consummate, sovereign, irresistible weed.

*

Sundance the cat will no doubt be your first concern, as he will insist upon being fed.

Who is this dark lover come calling, this inky maharajah
behind whom the underbrush is a palisade
of blackberry and goldenrod? Black as the lips of silence,
it's Sundance, strolling his minimalist grove,
fifteen red maples and three white pines,
eighteen dryads dancing on the barbered grass,
a three-dimensional frieze on an animate urn.
He called this morning with a gift in his mouth—
a vole, clasping and unclasping the shadow
in its elf-gray hand. Who's feeding whom?
What's Sundance's first concern? Unsettling
how much (the front door shut between us)
his cry of triumph sounded like a howl of pain.

*

What things so ever ye desire, when he pray, believe that ye receive them and ye shall have them.

Reviewing the troops on the shelves of the upstairs study:
Have You Felt Like Giving Up Lately? Are You Confused?
The Hunger for Reality. I can all but savor
the tang of the owner's convictions wafting from the pages.
Pencilled in the margin of *How to Pray*:
Prayers of two or more, when feeling
the same burden, are very strong.
And down in the living room, *Living in Step,*

Hey, I'm Alive!, *The Total Woman*, *The Book of Trees*—
and what have we brought for sustenance?
One copy of *Chaos* and two *Rogets*.

*

All the plants will need watering. I will probably leave a few in the kitchen sink.

In baskets, basins, clay pots, plastic,
garden soil, potting soil, vermiculite, water,
huddled on benches, railings, tables,
lurking on windowsills, dangling from rafters,
blooming, drooping, lush, tubercular,
some under the weather (such as there is in here),
some bushy-tailed, fresh as a hothouse daisy—
yet all of them docile, self-deprecating,
hushed and trusting as if they were
expecting us (housebroken like them),
rich kin from the interior.

*

The pond looks pretty only after a big rainstorm. There are apparently no underground springs, despite what the builder told me.

Some pond—a crater in the grass with a bed of dusty mud-tiles
flaunting that valance of lavender mimulus,
a sort of dysfunctional rain-trap, a brontosaurus print,
an old war wound. And above, closing in on every side,
that siege of horse-mint and heal-all, speedwell, skullcap
and wild marjoram, flourishing pennants of purple and blue,
closing in like a legion of militant weeds.

*

Sundance is cutting through the maples, reconnoitering,
appraising with his pale-green non-euclidean eye
the lay of the land. Now he steps from the shadow
and lets the trees get on with it, reading the future

with their clairvoyant roots, praying to the dark star
at the heart of their darkness. Sunlight leaps
from his flank, a fusillade of shooting stars.

★

*Walden is blue at one time and green another, even from the same point
of view.*

Last night's rain has beaten the mimulus flat as a blanket,
the floor of the pond is weeds from shore to shore,
ripples of joe-pye weed and wild marjoram,
ghost-minnows of violet and lavender winking and flickering.
If I'd a mind, I'd walk across it.

★

Strange bird haranguing us from the evening wood,
one three-note measure echoed relentlessly
till even our obstinate hearts begin pounding in triplets.

2.

At the boundary, life blossoms.

This evening an apparition: a half-grown doe
emerging from the maples, sniffing and peering,
skirting the boundary, seeking a way out
as if our clearing were merely one bad patch
in some incomprehensible counterpane,
the breeze that kissed the dew from the dayflower's lips
one whiff of the whirlwind, one tatter
of that inscrutable turbulence we call weather.
At last the doe leaps over a clump of skullcap,
vanishing as eerily as she appeared, leaving
under the half-wild apple a cloud of gnats.
Not every cloud has a silver lining.

★

Bright red slash from the pine to the sumacs.
By the time you can say *cardinal*, he's gone,
lost in that rabble of green shadows next door.

★

And the builder said, Let there be clearing,
and behold! there was clearing up and clearing out,
there was lopping and cropping, there was
leveling and laying bare (save fifteen maples
and three half-grown pines spared by the builder's dozer).
And lo! an opening, a respite, a letup, a breather,
a break in the chaos, an island of tentative order
in a sea of disorder, absolution, acquittal, reprieve.

★

*Our horizon is never quite at our elbows. The thick wood is not just at
our door, nor the pond, but somewhat is always clearing, familiar and
worn by us, appropriated and fenced in some way, and reclaimed from
Nature.*

Down by the spruce a little crowd of weed-trees
squints in the morning light. It's sumac, stealing
from the selvage—*Rhus*. Some say from *rheo*, I run.
(A little clearing in time. No time to rest.
Just time to regroup, our nerves at full alert,
to rally the battle-scarred, call up the reserves.)

★

Jerry the lawn-man grins from the riding mower
like a tanker from his turret. He's retaken the clearing.
The spindling sumac grove lies lopped and scattered.
This spring, Jerry says, he took his kid mountain-climbing.
The little shaver's weed-whacking the timothy.
One reckless bead of sweat rappels down his brow.

*

Sundance has dropped another jewel on our stoop,
the head of a chipmunk cleanly severed, the tiniest
wound at the throat where a little life keeps oozing out.

*

*A butterfly stirring the air today in Peking can transform storm systems
next month in New York.*

We keep circling back like the lost
or the enchanted. Circling the thicket of memory,
we back into a clearing, fetch up by a windless pond
trembling like the doe, sniffing and peering.
One quivering leaf on that maple might set off a storm
in its hippocampus. One breath from our lips might send
a mower hurtling through this nursery of infant sumacs.
Not Leviathan but a butterfly engages the gears of creation.

*

Sort of a sortie, slipping past the outposts of abandon.
Under the pines, a family of raspberry blossoms
smiling behind their broad green hands. I draw one closer
to inspect. Like rubbing my finger on a slave girl's teeth.

*

After the rain, like homeless men from under a bush,
the slugs creep onto the flags to sun themselves
while Thoreau's unwashed ghost shuffles through the maples,
past the woodshed, pausing at the mulch-pail
(that furnace of decay) to warm his heart.

*

I confess that I have hitherto indulged very little in philanthropic enterprises.

Asked on his deathbed what he thought of the world to come:
One world at a time, he croaked, as deep in their sockets
the gray eyes flared that incandescent blue
like bolts of chicory blazing in the roadside dust.
One pond, one plot, one thimbleful of this world
offered that pinchpenny eremite quite enough,
who built his house from the boards of a squatter's shack.

★

I had to pay four dollars and twenty-five cents tonight, he to vacate at five tomorrow morning

with his wife and his bawling four-month daughter—
the infant Fitchburg Railroad (that last improvement)
having no further need of their services.

★

At six I passed him and his family on the road. One large bundle held their all,—bed, coffee-mill, looking-glass, hens,—all but the cat, she took to the woods

—which offered her barely enough of this world, or the next
(having yielded the last of her lives in a woodchuck trap).
No room at the pond for the luxury of guilt.

★

If I repent of anything, it is very likely to be my good behavior.

3.

The purpose of an orchestra
          is to organize those sounds
                    and hold them

to an assembled order
          in spite of the
                    "wrong note."

Down in the pit the pond lays down a ground-bass,
a drone of invisible bees. Out by the road
the chicory is crooning its indigo blues.
The catbird chimes in with a clumsy fugue,
never stumbling over the same note twice,
only a cat in quotes that black gnats hover round
as if to say "not quite." With that little black cap
it seems less like a song than a call to prayer.

★

I do have a compost pile behind the woodshed, if you feel so inclined.

Raking the hummock of compost down to the quick,
watching the pillbug skitter, the centipede race,
the termite lug her wings through the steaming humus,
the slug wave his glistening palps in the emptiness,
we saw the granddaddy of earthworms haul himself
laboriously like a wounded titan from the abyss,
a gash in his side from which the rancor leaked,
where the teeth of the rake sank through like the fangs of
          chaos.

It's time to shovel fresh greens down the throat of decay,
this morning's orange peel onto last year's beets,
winding diaphanous corn silk round ash-gray cobs,
scrambling the seasons, damn the stratigraphy,
tearing a hole in the darkness to let in the day.

★

Nothing but Sundance and myself, against
the cannonry of chaos, nothing to flourish
but our fine intentions. He armed to the teeth,
I with my *Who's Who of Weeds,*
marshaling the troops, inspecting the earthworks.

Nothing but the great black hunter and me
marching to the pipes of the border guard.

*

No tilling, dibbling, mulching, pruning,
plowing, planting, reaping, gleaning,
harrows, combines, herbicides—
save, every other Monday, one
weed-whip and one riding mower,
only that momentary setback.
Then Tuesday morning the weeds crank up
their tiny engines and resume
their mild affectionate forays.

No digging sticks, no fertility rites,
only the two of us now and then
tending our own improbable garden,
scattering in a rented bed
doubtful seed on dubious ground.
Then strolling out through that glorious crop
of plantain, yarrow, chickweed, bedstraw,
skullcap, heal-all, cinquefoil, sorrel,
fertilized with nothing more
or less than our unlikely love.

*

A white flash in the upper branches of the aspen,
a rataplan of leaves—and who should float down
onto the new-mown lawn but a red-tailed hawk
to shake out his ominous, archangelic wings,
baring those improbable pantaloons.

*

This system was robust. If you perturbed it slightly, as any natural system is slightly perturbed by noise, the strangeness would not go away.

Small noise, the snarl of the mower, the catbird's mew,
the robin's mantra: *me! me! me!*
addressed to whomever it might concern.
(There are, after all, other systems yet more strange
where, should you let the moth of a whisper slip
past your clenched teeth, all is irrevocably lost.)
Strange but robust, robust yet exquisitely strange,
the outlandish biomechanics of the birds,
the maggoty dynamics of a compost pile,
a pond of flowers, a garden lush with weeds.

★

The ants have sent their aphids out to graze
by the pond (on the giddy pasture of a cottonwood leaf)
while the beetles keep munching and humping on the rose
and the sumacs flaunt their unlikely parasols
while Sundance sleeps inside on the easiest chair
and the asters carry on with their weedy amours,
while the bee-balm gossips with a potted fern
through the living-room window and the sun rains down
volley on volley of ultraviolet fire.

★

Sundance comes round to have a word (it sounds like
Now!)—leaps onto the bench, a couple of brotherly jabs
with his head in my ribs, then he settles beside me
to contemplate his kingdom.

★

Not only is it improbable that the "way back" can be found; as speciation increases, the possibility decreases that any new route can be found.

Time to pack up our tiny allotment of chaos,
time to retreat in earnest, time to go home,

for turbulence breeds its own improbable order
and the way back and ahead are one and the same.
We take our clearings when and where we find them,
and leave them when we go to their own devices,
a few gifts pressed in a book like schoolgirl keepsakes,
dried and flattened, etiolated, priceless.

from *The Yale Review*

The Printer's Error

◇ ◇ ◇

Fellow compositors
and pressworkers!

I, Chief Printer
Frank Steinman,
having worked fifty-seven
years at my trade,
and served for five years
as president
of the Holliston
Printers' Council,
being of sound mind
though near death,
leave this testimonial
concerning the nature
of printers' errors.

First: I hold that
all books and all
printed matter have
errors, obvious or no,
and that these are
their most significant moments,
not to be tampered with
by the vanity and folly
of ignorant, academic
textual editors.
Second: I hold that there are

three types of errors, in ascending
order of importance:
One: chance errors
of the printer's trembling hand
not to be corrected incautiously
by foolish scholars
and other such rabble
because trembling is part
of divine creation itself.
Two: silent, cool sabotage
by the printer,
the manual laborer
whose protests
have at times taken this
historical form,
covert interferences
not to be corrected
censoriously by the hand
of the second and far
more ignorant saboteur,
the textual editor.
Three: errors
from the touch of God,
divine and often
obscure corrections
of whole books by
nearly unnoticed changes
of single letters
sometimes meaningful but
about which the less said
by preemptive commentary
the better.
Third: I hold that all three
sorts of error,
errors by chance,
errors by workers' protest,
and errors by
God's work,
are in practice the
same and indistinguishable.

Therefore I,
Frank Steinman,
typographer
for thirty-seven years,
and cooperative Master
of the Holliston Guild
eight years,
being of sound mind and body
though near death
urge the abolition
of all editorial work
whatsoever
and manumission
from all textual editing
to leave what was
as it was, and
as it became,
except insofar as editing
is itself an error, and

therefore also divine.

from *The Stud Duck*

For a Brother

◇   ◇   ◇

When I was young, there was a song that went,
"I told you that I love you, now get out."
Last night, drunk at my party, you knocked over
the gas grill and blackened swordfish, you lout,
then tried to feel up my neighbor's daughter.
You sick rantallion, you phone at four a.m.
with a new joke, or to brag, or to beg for a loan.

Young, I didn't know what that song meant.
It just seemed funny. Today I am
bone tired of the crude fraternal weight
of your old bullying, you jackalone,
you sack of black rats' balls, you tank of piss.
And yet I love you, and so I must wait
until you're dead before I publish this.

from *North American Review*

Salutations to Fernando Pessoa

◇ ◇ ◇

Everytime I read Pessoa I think
I'm better than he is I do the same thing
more extravagantly—he's only from Portugal,
I'm American greatest Country in the world
right now End of XX Century tho Portugal
had a big empire in the 15th century never mind
now shrunk to a Corner of Iberian peninsula
whereas New York take New York for instance
tho Mexico City's bigger N.Y.'s richer think of Empire State
Building not long ago world empire's biggest skyscraper—
be that as't may I've experienced 61 years' XX Century
Pessoa walked down Rua do Ouro only till 1936
He entered Whitman so I enter Pessoa no
matter what they say besides dead he wouldn't object.

What way'm I better than Pessoa?
Known on 4 Continents I have 25 English books he only 3
his mostly Portuguese, but that's not his fault—
U.S.A.'s a bigger Country
merely 2 Trillion in debt a passing freakout,
Reagan's dirty work an American Century aberration
unrepresenting our Nation Whitman sang in Epic manner
tho worried about in Democratic Vistas
As a Buddhist not proud my superiority to Pessoa
I'm humble Pessoa was nuts big difference,
tho apparently gay—same as Socrates,
consider Michelangelo DaVinci Shakespeare
inestimable comrado Walt
True I was tainted Pinko at an early age a mere trifle

Science itself destroys ozone layers this era antiStalinists
poison entire earth with radioactive anticommunism
Maybe I lied somewhat
rarely in verse, only protecting others' reputations
Frankly too Candid about my mother tho meant well
Did Pessoa mention his mother? she's interesting,
powerful to birth sextuplets
Alberto Cairo Alvaro de Campos Ricardo Reis Bernardo Soares
        & Alexander Search simultaneously
with Fernando Pessoa himself a classic sexophrenic
Confusing personae not so popular
outside Portugal's tiny kingdom (till recently a secondrate police state)
Let me get to the point er I forget what it was
but certainly enjoy making comparisons between this Ginsberg
        & Pessoa
people talk about in Iberia hardly any books in English
presently the world's major diplomatic language extended throughout
        China.
Besides he was a shrimp, himself admits in interminable "Salutations
        to Walt Whitman"
Whereas 5′ 7½″ height
somewhat above world average, no immodesty,
I'm speaking seriously about me & Pessoa.
Anyway he never influenced me, never read Pessoa
before I wrote my celebrated "Howl" already translated into 24
        languages,
not to this day's Pessoa influence an anxiety
Midnight April 12 88 merely glancing his book
certainly influences me in passing, only reasonable
but reading a page in translation hardly proves "Influence."
Turning to Pessoa, what'd he write about? Whitman,
(Lisbon, the sea etc.) method peculiarly longwinded,
diarrhea mouth some people say—Pessoa Schmessoa.

from *The Threepenny Review*

PETER GIZZI

Another Day on
the Pilgrimage

◇ ◇ ◇

There is an I in space, I am, space
where a sparrow falls. Who can tell it?
Mix the scales and find a seam,
insert yourself waist-high.
When good-bye is the operative word
forgiveness is either easy or impossible.
Looking into your eyes I see more
than I came to address. The morning
the car lit out. That first memory
each time I die. Then is the world shut down
for a while. Hoping to meet again
some other day, hoping for the refrain
to conduct us all into a neighborhood
not furtive, but rich with color
and the telling of lost cities they leave never.
Place, this generating question
only answered when the orange drops,
that is twilight, becomes a kiss.

What are those sounds in the dark?
Can they tell of our lives, can they
begin to unfold the pain in the eye,
the slow girth of the long night.
There are crowds gathered with faces

pressed up against the sill, so many
faces at the sill. I wish I could tell them
what we are and where we are going.
Instead the blue interval and the open plain,
this green wedge and the brown hill.
Tell me, can I say *who* or can I
say *now*? And will words awaken
the desire to know, to push open the nerve.
The green book on the blue bed has answers.
It tells of our need for description, the apex
where nerve net and hair stem meet
and expose wind or express time between
the sheets. I have a paper cut on my finger
it smarts when I push off to feed. Turn
the page to diagram 4, a box and an outline
of a cape, together they articulate—grain,
thorn and shoes—they equal a figure.
Tiresias on an open road reading signs.
The dead are useful he said
to tell us where we are. This is a hard hat area.
The image of the spectator trapped
in a mirror, the relationship of spectator, object
and the space within love's bent axis.

Will you quit that banging?
Like a sullen barber the blade of the season
mows down the last buds and you find yourself
without pajamas. The balloon ascends
throughout the years and the view
only gets less colorful and distant. O where
are my tin toys and first books and the sun
is no longer new? The pages of the book are smooth
and yet you can climb the face of narrative
carefully and with great ardor. The one flower
on the cliff face will be yours if you persist.

The wind continues to interpret the story
as the old latch is gone from the back door—
whoosh and bang all evening
makes one's nerves sharpen to the point
of a syringe. I like how autobiography is geologic
or geographical. All my people have larger bodies.
Will you compare me to a pyramid or a clover
in the trash? When I am inscribed to tell
of the beauty of innuendo
I am like unto a feather—giddy and quick.

When the skiff returns from its solo
each night the organism is renewed.
Nameless moments our destiny.
So many leaves to unfurl. Later to be
reinscribed in a second tongue
we call grammar, we call and call forever
to the next page. The speech in boxes.
Little caskets of ventriloquism tell
our plight, explain our confusion
and generally identify our loneliness here
on the surface. What it was would be
like this. How small and how nothing.
Cathedral light only in memory.
Immemorial space smiles, blurs
the template before the impression
is made. The artifact in time fades
and we are left with a blank slate.
We are left, it is that simple.

The robes lie in a rebus on the shore
where the beloved sang,
thwarted into nothing. Thwarted.
No embellishment please, the day
is sufficient. Who could tell, as all

the listeners' ears are stoppered with their
own invention. A carbuncle ascends
like a gray morning is a body?
The opium eaters have erased their eyelids.
An absorbed earth is altered, fallow
and gusts of stinging filth pierce us
as we move from moment to task.
Later the voice stripped laughter's heft
and became a mottled chronology.
You haven't moved an inch. *Know it.*
Twirl. Until drawing all rumor
into your coterie you exhaust the actual
breeze which is our inheritance, not
the small fires you, squatting, tend.
Right activity is the only promise
twinned with the natural processes of earth.
That's where you can find me,
carrying my bundle for the pyre?

O road. Sing the changes your geometry gives.
Recondite lines projecting
into revisionist fields at dawn.
A wobbling moon imitates a mouth
in mourning. These gestures caught in blue light
become a context become carved upon
all features enacted in sleep.
A tiny voice has begun to sing the background
of everything the foreground blurs.
Ecstatic in its trill and because we seek
less and settle for more its swell
will burst us in our distracted way,
our mortgaged fear, adumbrated in kind.

from *apex of the M*

Asparagus

◇ ◇ ◇

The day my father calls to say he'll buy
six cemetery lots, I'm putting in asparagus.
So many? I ask (those empty rooms he calls from,
the empty napkin rings). We don't want her lonely,
he says. But I'll be fire. I'll be ash.
You never know, he says. Here I am, a six-foot trench,
I'm in it, knee-deep, digging.

White asparagus. Sweet, stringy mushroom
you tend at night. By moonlight, you reach
under the earth to slice it clean.
The nights before the war, my mother danced
with barons who smoked short cigarettes.
The shoes she wore shone silver like the moon,
and Gypsies read her palm.

Here, it's all grown green. *Asparagrass*
read roadstand signs. Lily-of-the-valley overran
her patch, leaving only one green finger to rise
each spring. My mother's wedding band was gold
as butter. Before each meal, she bowed for grace,
hands poking up toward God.

Look, she says, asparagus. The day stretches long,
most of it spent on trains. We rock against
our bags, traveling north in the country my mother

still calls hers. Does she notice that it's fall?
There isn't much to see—mounded earth, inedible
moot points. Her finger taps the window long after
the view has changed.

from *The Yale Review*

ELTON GLASER

Undead White European Male

◇ ◇ ◇

for Charles Simic

Profile like the Barrymores
On a bad hair day; rebarbative sighs
From the borsalino and the opera cloak;
Duet of the dogteeth, pitched high against
The lovelorn seizure of his smile—

Laszlo, victim of insomnia
Boxed out from the sun, too tired for all these
Retroactive ironies of blood. Ah, Laszlo,
Six hundred years of training
And still missing the shift
From buried body to bat, still turning up
As finch or butterfly, as two pieces of black bread
Hinged on a clot of jam.

Laszlo with a taste for Italian,
And a garlic allergy. Laszlo of the snows,
More lonely than
The Winter Queen of Bohemia
In a season of chapped lips,
Putting the frostbite on another frightened neck.

It's not true that evil
Comes easier than good—too much
Upkeep on the formal sleepwear,

Too many forced landings
Through a closed pane, or hard against
The muddy ruckus of a pig shed.

And these nights, when the dry and aromatic
Red of the jugular
Pulses like a warning light,
Even the connoisseurs can't tell
Without a test
Who's safe to siphon or decant.

Aristocrat of the crypt, scholar *cum laude*
In the I.V. League, Laszlo would rather
Paddle his blue blood
Down some twisted river in the tropics,
Part piranha, part parakeet, or lift himself
To the moon, cape held out stiff behind him,
Windsurfing on the Sea of Tranquillity.

More Parisian than parasite, he'd much prefer
To sink in a boudoir of silk and pearls
Than pierce some punk
With tattoos poisoned on the throat, or drain those
Schoolgirls in their Catholic skirts
Cut one prepubescent inch above the knee.

Exarchs and bishops
And other salesmen of the spirit's need
Mean less to him
Than the pale omens of anemia,
Though he'll swoon
Each evening when the swamps release
A smear of mosquitoes, the thin
Whir of their wings like a dentist's drill,
Fat males lazing on the breeze
While their women
Shop for dinner with a sharp snoot.

Saint of the satin afterlife,
Anti-Narcissus of the vacant mirror,
Gypsy myth
Feeding on the tangled branches of a dream,

Laszlo goes down
To the dark rout of émigrés
Barred back across the border,
A spray of shadows
Not made welcome in this world
Afraid of its own past, ashamed to inherit
That west in which
The same sun that sets on them
Sets him forever free.

from *The Gettysburg Review*

A Still Life,
Symbolic of Lines

◇ ◇ ◇

It's aesthetically lovely, but pangs the mind
—the way in Aubrey's *Lives* the whole of sixty, seventy years
is fit in one well-loaded line. Of Sir Jonas Moore:
Sciatica: he cured it by boyling his Buttock. And so
those anguished nights, the days of frenzied panacea-shopping,
go by in eight words. Or of Mary Rich, countess of Warwick:
Shee needed neither to borrow Shades, nor reflexive Lights,
to set her off, being personally great in all naturall Endowments,
click. One day there won't even be Aubrey around, just
dust in skirling threads through the silicon chips, and then
even these relict lines will be gone, will be mulch,
will be dander hoarded by ants. I've tried to do it today

with my father: one line. But I can't choose. *Since his work day*
was 12 hours, it compressed his love for his family,
in the remaining hours, past their understanding. That's
a real possibility: for truth, if not for eloquence. (Or
more than 12: up all night, in that basement "study"
—one desk, over the drain hole—where the nickels
for our bargain-table shoes and our sweaters from "seconds"
    stores
were fossicked out of his leather-look plastic ledger books.)
He'd put on his salesman's smile the way somebody else might
pin on a badge of great office—that's also, I think,
a contender. But you'd have to have known my father
to appreciate these, while Aubrey's prose makes strangers

clear. Isaac Barrow: *He was a strong man, but*
pale as the Candle he studyed by. Or: *In love with Geometry . . .,*
Thomas Hobbes . . . *was wont to draw lines on his thigh*
and on the sheets, abed. I'm reading Aubrey back at the house
my seventy-six-year-old mother still lives in—reading him,
one of the few books that I've brought for the week I'm
  helping her
post-surgery heal, dampened gauzy strip by gauzy strip.
He's good on suffering: *To Cure the Tooth-Ach, Take a new Nail,*
and make the Gum bleed with it, and then drive it into an Oak.
This did cure Sir William Neal's Son, when he was Mad with
  the Pain.
But really: it's time to close that book, it's time
to face each stitch in my mother, and start to learn the lesson

of pain: how something inside us not even the size
of a fish egg clouds the ceiling of this crackerbox house
with thick gray wafts of lamentation, and funnels
into the sour, cul-de-sac shadow in the toe of a shoe.
It's time to change the pads again, and freshen the salves.
It's time to retrace—reravel—the trails of thingness in this place
where I was raised, and where his presence is a lingering,
ghost-swirled weather. Things: the Bible
in its silver filigree cover; the yuk-yuk naughty
heads-or-tails coin still "hidden" under his handkerchiefs;
the dime-store pie safe (one-ply tin) with dings by now
as acute as the lunar surface. . . . Remember *Plotto*?

—"a thick, expensive book containing brief, algebraic
descriptions of every possible story construction
known to mankind." In the 30s and 40s, writers for the pulps
resorted regularly to its riches. All the plotlines
extended as niftily as if a surveyor had done them;
what you simply had to do was add persuasive *objets*,
a treasure map, an obsidian idol, a smoking purse-size gun,
at the lines' conjunctions. And here, in the house
of my own small history?—his rubberbanded note cards
with the names of clients A to Z, his *Kiddush* cup
for the ritual wine, his cheap police-band radio . . .
persuasive *objets*. And surely if I were sensitive enough

to these, the narrative of who he was, and who my mother is,
would boldly write itself across the air, with a clarity
and a finality beyond question. Of course it doesn't work
that way. I rummage and muddle. Tonight I sit
at his desk in the basement. The desk is a dark and dull pea-green
(the office surplus color of 1955), and so is the 40 watts down here,
and the splattered blotter—murkily, khakily dingy.
Nearly shouting out from all this is the gummyish pink
of his old friends and saviours—the lozenge kind
for pencil, and the flat disc kind for ink, things phasing
right now out of cultural use themselves. A still life, symbolic
of lines; of lines and their erasure.

from *Southwest Review*

The description of *Plotto* is from Lee Server's *Danger Is My Business*. John Aubrey:
"How these curiosities would be quite forgott, did not such idle fellowes as I am putt
them downe."

Being Pharaoh

◊ ◊ ◊

My grandmother turned into an old man,
deaf, with a hairy chin. It is August,

the damp panting of nights—I am
gradually building my own underworld

not just with prospective grief but
wires to hold up the asphodels.

Into it, a whole migration of shapes
skinned by light, pears gone

flat, and cars, and shadow like a floored heart.
They're the file of a river

and the Greeks had a river, the Romans.
The Egyptians who civilized the dead.

Tonight I am sick of every man
and his past. And the past is tired of his

request that it love him. I am trying
to make my bed. I am trying to keep

an angel from cracking my hip. The moon's
sleeve is flipped back in a drawer . . .

Thrush, you little singing spade—
I'm an unforgivably domestic mourner

and I might sleep through someone's
late supper, or hunger, just think how

oblivious he will be. While I am in
the dark rustling my own inventory:

Each time we fall out of love we
say it wasn't really love at all as if,

landing, a plane would say *no, not
actual sky*. While I am in the dark

getting fit for an afterlife. Admit
we never know the difference, like the woman

who stands up in the cinema and becomes
the black keyhole we peer into. I am

trying to keep her head down. So long
even her mother and mother's mother

turn blue. I am trying to keep
the ancestors out of the bedroom

so I can conceive a new face and new
arms, the feather trees across

the river, the curious shore dog.
Keep the distance simple like the top

deck of the parking garage from which
we can see the hospital. The present

may bond to any molecule, future
or past: My parents were kissing

while someone dragged the body past
the doorway, bag zipped to the chin

on the gurney, the head wound in white gauzes.
My father had taken off his mask, still

hissing oxygen, and Mother was bent.
Of all things I've seen it was

old love that kept them from seeing.
Beautiful discretion, what moment will you

save from me? This should have been
a dream, something to wake from

but I never do. I am trying.
I will be pharaoh yet—

sealed with tiny boats and slavish
figurines. I am sick of every face

floating a sex by itself. Take in
this lampshade and these

curtains. Objects are memory.
As a child I pictured the soul as a glass

wing, fluted, gelatinous, detached
as my voice under water. I made it up

a body—a paperweight—no snow
in the water, no water under the earth,

no music ever again in my hair, after
my hair. The dead will point to it,

What was the name for this, point to my hand,
What was the name for this? One life

has been mine so long, streets
and bicycles, monuments

descend in it. In the bedroom a shirt
has fallen on shoes. Keep me

from seeing: Moon wanting into the dark
like the torn from—

the photograph—
It is August. One woman is so long

longing does not come out of her.
But this time I have loved you

so long I become
the boy you were. I must still

be alive, for everything is changing and
incomplete. Half a tree, half

drives its shadowy web near the shutters.
August has just turned September. The ancestors

want 4,000-year-old grain, hard as quartz,
in grain jars. All I have are cigarettes.

What a night this is. What a night.
I'll lie down and my pillow will thrum

like a machine. I'll go barefoot
to the window, see if any light is

still on in any house. Who else
is afraid of missing something. Who else

knows one thing God can't enter
is my memory: I, a minor

twentieth century poet, the first
of September, 4 a.m., finish one thing.

from *Field*

LAURENCE GOLDSTEIN

Permissive Entry:
A Sermon on Fame

◇　◇　◇

Life is porous enough
for any number of interventions:
a directory's worth of neighbors,
sales personnel, colleagues disputing
Endymion or *Wonderland*, the sexpot on Channel 2;
at the margins of consciousness
the junk-mail, or noise, of
infinite presences grind their unrecorded
deeds, as if mere activity mattered.

One can grant them valuable life
they hardly deserve, like Bernstein
in *Citizen Kane* who lets a pretty passer-by
haunt his autumnal reveries; she's
the softer spirit he sacrificed to Kane.
Bernstein or Goldstein, Mankiewicz or Welles,
who hasn't, if only from perversity, kept
some indulgent memory of a rose-lipped beauty,
a face for the lost happiness of life?

Biographies seldom tell us this. Letters
may do so: candid, egocentric, shameless,
they reveal the poet in August 1945 worried
exclusively about an acquaintance's sour review
in a Cleveland daily, how the McCarthy terror
went unnoticed by an actress who fumed at extras

or daydreamed of an admiral. . . . Decades afterward
we circulate to flesh and blood over a fine dessert
the contagious novelty of such dated gossip.

It's more than the wary glance at the watering hole;
some arbitrary fame we envy, and cherish,
the incidental unearned influence
that outlasts a mother's devotion, as a bon mot
may be all we remember of a friendship.
Blame it on timepieces, masscom, aging,
this reflex salute to some Bulkington,
nothing more than a shape washed overboard
to float, but never quite sink, in the circumambient flood.

Like the South African who chattered
one July evening in 1961, on a crowded cargo boat
plying between Brindisi and Haifa, planning
his post-adolescent return to Johannesburg
after seven years of sowing wild oats.
"That's an awful place," one heckler said
and he rejoined, "We're all traveling to our separate hells."
Whoever he is, and wherever, he would never believe
how often his overheard remark has braced me in solitude.

The vitality of chance utterance
is reason enough for art, a mirror & medium of
permissive entry into the universe of lives.
Like Thoreau we occasionally lop off
fluent humanity and "center" ourselves, grow bored,
set off on the Concorde, inviting strangers
to impact upon us, and write them briefly down.
Each is an imaginable subject,
a minor note in the swelling music of ourselves.

Some in every generation
obsess all contemporaries; others must settle for less,
celebrities only to a few. So what? Enough to
impinge like . . . there! . . . two terriers capering by,
performing our walk-ons for no special audience,
while summoning to alert attention

now and tomorrow, the Elect our wistful voices
strain at, less and less audibly, echoes
of all castaways gone into the deep.

from *Tampa Review*

If So

◇ ◇ ◇

    I give you the unhingeing sleeve
dropped the seam   it went onto our back
was fodderless

    wilted say by the gravel road
who ran a mile with legs apart   to the unrailed post
    neck hanging over the cliff
groupless   the adored single urges

the bird shadow crossing the room   "leave the outdoors"
earns a pittance of food on the ledge with the mother
of ten eggs   I thought the real bird was feeding on ices
  the shadow was ten eggs   I learned.

do you wonder if a run on sand is better than inside
does this strike you as shallow   does it tease aloud the action is
   part of a wing   the main house is wallowing

the building was added it grew from an arm   protruded out of the
      thigh
averred the upper terrace grew up fighting   is divided.

    to think of you turned inside   your garment rent
your garment rent you are appointed   apart from the rites your value
         lessens as in a daring scheme

you are beheaded
much cast out that rolls on the ground   toss out the wool and the
    thread
of what worked   it doesn't last and correctly untongued   thought to
compete   how you work or unlearn   if so tell me.

from *Princeton University Library Chronicle*

Days of 1992

◇ ◇ ◇

"Pray for the souls of the antisemites."
ALFRED CORN, "Somerset Alcaics"

I spent the morning waxing the furniture,
thick orange beeswax sprayed on a chamois-cloth,
    dull glow on what was flat and dusty,
      odor of beeswax, a tinge of honey.

Storm-crumbled plaster, storm-swollen window frames:
work for the bookish Orthodox carpenter;
    then a discussion with the plumber
      who will dismantle the bathtub Thursday.

Low, heavy clouds, unbroken humidity
(like Great Lakes gray in darkest America)
    makes indoors smell like dirty linen.
      Open the windows! Invite the breeze in!

If it were Sunday, I'd do my market run
Boulevard Richard Lenoir: half-past nine I'd
    be filling up my wicker basket,
      bathed in the polyglot cries of vendors.

Chard, onions, eggplant, cherries and strawberries,
écru pleurotes, their undersides filigreed
    to be sauteed with breast of chicken?
      Trout? Or a skate wing (black butter, capers).

But it's not Sunday, only a workaday
Tuesday, after the bleak anniversary:
    my chosen people gave my people
    up to the brown-shirted blond invaders.

One generation, now, since the war stories.
Since the betrayals, since the internment camps,
    since the haggard few survivors
    got off the trains that had damned, then saved them,

just to confront revisionist bureaucrats.
As I live out my chosen diaspora
    watching the clouds and writing letters,
    what earthly good is my faceless mourning?

I went for a message in rue Rambuteau
from a wiry, bearded Jew in his sixties
    born two streets over from his office.
    He and his parents endured the war years

hiding out in a village in Périgord.
More lucky than two-thirds of their relatives,
    they never saw a single German.
    "If we'd stayed here, I would not be here now."

What did my neighbors do when the gendarmes came
Jew-hunting in this Jewish arrondissement?
    I've never asked my next-door neighbor:
    frail centenarian who was fifty-

two then, a few years older than I am, now.
I'm frightened to investigate memories:
    maybe she liked Pétain, perhaps she
    told the gendarmes where a man was hiding,

maybe she knew no Jews, ignored the buses,
maybe she hid a scared Jewish girl in her
    dank Turkish toilet on the landing
    until an aunt with forged papers fetched her.

So I invent her, paint her with politics
past, while she follows soaps on her TV set,
  cleans, totes her bread and wine upstairs, feeds
  sparrows in the Place des Vosges dry bread crumbs,

reads daily papers, rightish and populist.
I wait to hear the Sécu come check on her
  mornings. She's a background music to my
  life for eight years here: how much longer?

She goes, and I go, into our histories
as the century's flame-darkened ending
  silences us if we've stayed silent,
  letting the cries of the street subsume us.

from *Colorado Review*

St. Peregrinus' Cancer

◇ ◇ ◇

His miracles abbreviated, *Lives of Saints*
    Elaborates his pain;
The famous field he crossed, obliquely, like a crab.
    Silver-pointed crickets
Fanned away, hiding from his dogwood stick,
    His cap on auburn grass.
The clover smelled of local wine, and there
    His vanity could end.

The caption, "Byzantine and mediterranean,"
    Appeared in my edition
As "Bizarre and sweaty." He was bizarre and sweaty
    Crossing the field in pain.
The parables he hoped the baffled children would
    Recite turned back to babble.

And grass *was not unlike* his doubt, scorched and growing.
    Not silent or silenced,
Nor what in such despair would silence silence—translated
    "He liked to be alone."
An audience today would understand. He went
    The other way; his name
Meant "crossing the field"; going away, one-legged
    In wild licorice.

He sneezed, ruining his pretty suffering,
    The patron saint of cancer.
Once I asked for his crisis, tattooed on my thigh.

A conversation piece,
Approachable: "Hello. I see by your thigh
    You want to be alone."

Or "Haven't we met? I know your thigh is not unlike
    My own . . . . ." A mock-romantic
Brutalism: faux-enameled navel rings.
    And then declare "Cut here,"
For tattooed dotted lines; the latest cloisonné
    Engraved in skin, *"my love."*
My mother chronicled her cobalt, chemo,
    Then tamoxifen.

Her years of this; her " *'Bravery,'* the doctors said."
    We picked at crab imperials.
I wished for more. I couldn't help it, imagining
    A swoon in cold moiré
Have and overcome, have and overcome,
    And then I did. I had

The diagnosis; surgery accomplished; stitches,
    Pink-stemmed flushes,
Shades of plasma; doubled burgundies and dusky
    Roses; weltered flesh;
The mottled violets and flattened mauve corsages;
    Burnt sienna tissue;
Hardy musk and moss maroon; Madame de Pompadour,
    Ancestor rose! We laughed,

A ladies' lunch, where overarcing hats with velvet
    Clover met; a field
I'd never seen before, the undulating veils
    Of air and grass became
"You're thin, so thin, so thin, so thin, so thin," so then,
    We were alike, at last.

from *Western Humanities Review*

Prospects

◇ ◇ ◇

We have set out from here for the sublime
Pastures of summer shade and mountain stream;
I have no doubt we shall arrive on time.

Is all the green of that enamelled prime
A snapshot recollection or a dream?
We have set out from here for the sublime

Without provisions, without one thin dime,
And yet, for all our clumsiness, I deem
It certain that we shall arrive on time.

No guidebook tells you if you'll have to climb
Or swim. However foolish we may seem,
We have set out from here for the sublime

And must get past the scene of an old crime
Before we falter and run out of steam,
Riddled by doubt that we'll arrive on time.

Yet even in winter a pale paradigm
Of birdsong utters its obsessive theme.
We have set out from here for the sublime;
I have no doubt we shall arrive on time.

from *The New Yorker*

Unearthly Voices

(Hofmannsthal at the Monastery of St. Luke)

◇ ◇ ◇

Wind tumbles the branches by the side of the road
and tiny clouds sail across a blistered sky.

Twilight in blue mountains, a bow-shaped valley
at the end of the world, one gashed pine

and a monk wading up to the waist in briar-roses.
Here at last, dismounting, a worldly traveler

shakes off three days' dust and stretches his legs
on the eternal path. He follows a black gown

through a door carved into the mountain's flesh,
crosses an enclosed garden and enters a space

where a flame burns perpetually under the Holy Virgin.
Was this where the gods became the Lord Almighty?

He unpacks; he drinks clear water from a fountain;
he hears the unaccompanied voices of men rising

and falling inside a church, nearby but also far
from lamentation or desire. Why had he come

except to slip through the cloisters like a ghost
listening to Gregorian chants—signals from another world—

to smell the incense and honey that load the air
and contemplate the humility of kneeling

at Vespers, or lying on a stone-cold floor
in the early morning, or standing in meditation?

Why had he come except to prove to himself
that he could never be one of them? Suddenly

he hears a woman's tremulous voice glorying
from an open window, faithful, chanting,

and a second voice echoing hers, insubstantial,
as if the mysteries had borrowed a human breast

for singing, and then a third voice rising
beyond the others, a messenger whose flare gleams

over the walls of a darkened orchard, the cloudy
depths of a ruined city. . . . The singing stops

and a smooth face appears at the window, a novice
whose hair falls across his shoulders to his waist.

The choirboys whisper together in the courtyard.
Tomorrow he leaves for Athens, but tonight

he is gazing at a thousand-year-old olive grove
that grows over broken columns, climbing the stairs

and standing on a balcony between two fig trees,
watching the evening star punctual over the mountains.

Now and then a light ascends, as if from water:
the shepherds keeping warm under a lonely crescent.

He peers into the darkness as into a cistern
and feels the centuries welling up beneath him.

An Unnamable is present, the Unreachable exists
in shuddering sheep-bells and loud cicadas,

in dogs barking at each other across the hills,
answering questions, piercing the night's skin,

in stars blazing like torches, one by one,
on the earthly horizon. He lies down

on a cot—he will not sleep—and hears
church bells flecking the snow-capped mountains,

far from home, somewhere near Delphi, and then
angels waking in the treetops, and owls calling

to wolves howling far away. Candles waver,
bodies flicker through the windy corridors

and soon they are praying and singing, kneeling
in adoration before an absolute presence, God,

the unfathomable One. He turns over and listens
to voices floating unearthly over the rooftops. . . .

He drifts toward his family in another country,
almost in another century, on a different floor

of the dream. He broods: a stranger who visits
an ancient monastery is a tourist of eternity.

He believes nothing. He sees himself walking
on a narrow path, alone between bare mountains

while a single sparrow-hawk circles overhead
and an icy stream threads its way underground.

He passes into the shade of a gigantic rock
as angels disappear into cypresses and stone-pines.

The silence is wide and overwhelming, calm
blanket of oblivion, peacefulness of death. . . .

At daybreak the voices begin again, ringing out
the darkness, bringing back the sun.

from TriQuarterly

Against the Literal

◇　◇　◇

Of course each shrub and rodent has a name, sometimes more than one,
and every weed and every flower and all the sonorous trees,

and the winds too, their mistrals and siroccos and easts and wests,
but I am telling you to keep them from me a moment: if the gray jay

and the pinyon jay are the same, I don't need to know yet,
and I most want to get rid of Latin binomials. We are entering

new country. If I see the same squirrel five times, must I know
there is one peripatetic, curious little animal, or may I believe

the woods are teeming with squirrels? The sun is brighter
here than anywhere else: I don't care if the altitude provides a logical

explanation; it's brighter just now for other reasons. Observe:
the flowers here have more seductive fragrances. If I were to think

your voice carries especially far because I always hear it,
or that the camp robber takes bread from my hand for reasons other

than greed, would it trouble you not to disabuse me? I'm not saying
forever. Long enough. A moment.

from *The Georgia Review*

Seventeen

◇ ◇ ◇

Ahead of me, the dog reared on its rope,
and swayed. The pickup took a hard left turn,
and the dog tipped off the side. He scrambled, fell,
and scraped along the hot asphalt
before he tumbled back into the air.
I pounded on my horn and yelled. The rope
snapped and the brown dog hurtled into the weeds.
I braked, still pounding on my horn. The truck
stopped too.

        We met halfway, and stared
down at the shivering dog, which flinched
and moaned and tried to flick its tail.
Most of one haunch was scraped away
and both hind legs were twisted. *You stupid shit!*
I said. He squinted at me. "Well now, bud—
you best watch what you say to me."
I'd never cussed a grown-up man before.
I nodded. I figured on a beating. He grinned.
"You so damn worried about that ole dog,
he's yours." He strolled back to his truck,
gunned it, and slewed off, spraying gravel.
The dog whined harshly.

        By the road,
gnats rose waist-high as I waded through
the dry weeds, looking for a rock.
I knelt down by the dog—tail flick—
and slammed the rock down twice. The first

blow did the job, but I had planned for two.
My hands swept up and down again. I grabbed
the hind legs, swung twice, and heaved the dog
into a clump of butterfly weed and vetch.
But then I didn't know that they had names,
those roadside weeds. His truck was a blue Ford,
the dog a beagle. I was seventeen.
The gnats rose, gathered to one loose cloud,
then scattered through coarse orange and purple weeds.

from *The Southern Review*

T. R. HUMMER

Apocatastasis Foretold in the Shape of a Canvas of Smoke

◇ ◇ ◇

At the left edge of the field of vision, a stooped woman dumps
Steaming water from her galvanized bucket against a granite wall.
In this meditation, she might be an emblem of genocide

Or simply somebody's grandmother dumping dishwater in the snow.
Gray earth, gray sky—the brushstroke of the horizon visible
Only to someone who knows what to look for, pure

Transparent style. The water is a soapy broth of tea dregs,
Grease, and lye, which the wormy dog that hides
Under her skirt licks from the frozen stones—its every gesture

An archetype, something that could be perfectly described only
In Indo-European. In the middle distance, from the indistinct
Shadow of a minor mountain, there is hazy motion, possibly an army:

The sound of leather groaning, silk-muffled hammers
Of the temple builders, adze-chafe, pneumatic saws, the crack
Of a splintering axle-tree. The dog's ruff is the same shade of silver

As the galvanized zinc of her bucket, and the water the bucket holds,
And the vapor that rises off the frost-etched stone of the wall.
Her old dress bunches at her belly in an intaglio like stretch marks.

She had children, and those children died. She had children
And those children had children. Where is the nostalgia
For humanity? Where are all the stories we have learned

To interpret so perfectly? You may think there is tragedy here,
But this is only the beginning. In the gunpowder haze that lifts
Over the boundary-ridge, and in the bucket's mural of steam,

The characters gather: a man who lifts his handful of blood
To the vacuous spirit he knows is his mother, and she drinks
And speaks his name, and is oblivion. Look

Where the machinery of heaven drags form after form
Out of this sarcophagus God carved from the onyx cliff-face of being
And hinged with elaborate craftsmanship into the joinery of her spine,

So when the latch clicks and the lid of her body swings open,
Another rises luminous and whole into the expanse of unconcealment.
It comes almost to nothing. Winter is here and the half-starved

Cattle still give milk, though it is thin, with a tinge of vein-blue.
February sleet spits on flagstones with the noise a bronze knife makes
On hickory. The craftsman at his bench is carving another bowl

For goats' blood, while the dog in the culvert gnaws
Whatever rat he can find, then curls his carcass in on itself
Like a Möbius strip for warmth, everything drawn together.

from *Sewanee Theological Review*

All Wild Animals
Were Once Called Deer

◇ ◇ ◇

Some truck was gunning the night before up Pippin Hill's steep grade
And the doe was thrown wide. This happened five years ago now,
Or six. She must have come out of the woods by Simpson's red
      trailer—

The one that looks like a faded train car—and the driver
Did not see her. His brakes no good. Or perhaps she hit the truck.
That happens, too. A figure swims up from nowhere, a flying figure

That seems to be made of nothing more than moonlight, or vapor,
Until it slams its face, solid as stone, against the glass.
And maybe when this happens the driver gets out. Maybe not.

Strange about the kills we get without intending them.
Because we are pointed in the direction of something.
Because we are distracted at just the right moment, or the wrong.

We were waiting for the school bus. It was early, but not yet light.
We watched the darkness draining off like the last residue
Of water from a tub. And we didn't speak, because that was our way.

High up a plane droned, drone of the cold, and behind us the flag
In front of the Bank of Hope's branch trailer snapped and popped in
      the wind.
It sounded like a boy whipping a wet towel against a thigh

Or like the stiff beating of a swan's wings as it takes off
From the lake, a flat drumming sound, the sound of something
Being pounded until it softens, and then—as the wind lowered

And the flag ran out wide—there was a second sound,
    the sound of running fire.
And there was the scraping, too, the sad knife-against-skin scraping
Of the acres of field corn strung out in straggling rows

Around the branch trailer that had been, the winter before,
    our town's claim to fame
When, in the space of two weeks, it was successfully robbed twice.
The same man did it both times, in the same manner.

He had a black hood and a gun, and he was so polite
That the embarrassed teller couldn't hide her smile when he showed
        up again.
They didn't think it could happen twice. But sometimes it does.

Strange about that. Lightning strikes and strikes again.
My piano teacher watched her husband, who had been struck as a boy,
Fall for good, years later, when he was hit again.

He was walking across a cut cornfield toward her, stepping over
The dead stalks, holding the bag of nails he'd picked up at the
        hardware store
Out like a bouquet. It was drizzling so he had his umbrella up.

There was no thunder, nothing to be afraid of.
And then a single bolt from nowhere, and for a moment the man
Was doing a little dance in a movie, a jig, three steps or four,

Before he dropped like a cloth, or a felled bird.
This happened twenty years ago now, but my teacher keeps
Telling me the story. She hums while she plays. And we were
        humming

That morning by the bus stop. A song about boys and war.
And the thing about the doe was this. She looked alive.
As anything will in the half light. As even lawn statues will.

I was going to say as even children playing a game of statues will,
But of course they *are* alive. Though sometimes
A person pretending to be a statue seems farther gone in death

Than a statue does. Or to put it another way,
Death seems to be the living thing, the thing
That looks out through the eyes. Strange about that . . .

We stared at the doe for a long time and I thought about the way
A hunter slits a deer's belly. I've watched this many times.
And the motion is a deft one. It is the same motion the swan uses

When he knifes the children down by his pond on Wasigan Road.
They put out a hand. And quick as lit grease, the swan's
Boneless neck snakes around in a sideways circle, driving

The bill hard toward the softest spot . . . All those songs
We sing about swans, but they are mean. And up close, often ugly.
That old Wasigan bird is a smelly, moth-eaten thing,

His wings stained yellow as if he chewed tobacco,
His upper bill broken from his foul-tempered strikes.
And he is awkward, too, out of the water. Broken-billed and gaited.

When he grapples down the steep slope, wheezing and spitting,
He looks like some old man recovering from hip surgery,
Slowly slapping down one cursed flat foot, then the next.

But the thing about the swan is this. The swan is made for the water.
You can't judge him out of it. He's made for the chapter
In the rushes. He's like one of those small planes my brother flies.

Ridiculous things. Something a boy dreams up late at night
While he stares at the stars. Something a child draws.
I've watched my brother take off a thousand times, and it's always

The same. The engine spits and dies, spits and catches—
A spurting match—and the machine shakes and shakes as if it were
Stuck together with glue and wound up with a rubber band.

It shimmies the whole way down the strip, past the pond,
Past the wind bagging the goose-necked wind sock, past the banks
Of bright red and blue planes. And as it climbs slowly

Into the air, wobbling from side to side, cautious as a rock climber,
Putting one hand forward then the next, not even looking
At the high spot above the tree line that is the question,

It seems that nothing will keep it up, not a wish, not a dare,
Not the proffered flowers of our held breath. It seems
As if the plane is a prey the hunter has lined up in his sights,

His finger pressing against the cold metal, the taste of blood
On his tongue . . . but then, at the dizzying height
Of our dismay, just before the sky goes black,

The climber's frail hand reaches up and grasps the highest rock,
Hauling, with a last shudder, the body over,
The gun lowers, and perfectly poised now, high above

The dark pines, the plane is home free. It owns it all, *all*.
My brother looks down and counts his possessions,
Strip and grass, the child's cemetery the black tombstones

Of the cedars make on the grassy hill, the wind-scrubbed
Face of the pond, the swan's white stone. . . .
In thirty years, roughly, we will all be dead . . . That is one thing . . .

And you can't judge the swan out of the water. . . . That is another.
The swan is mean and ugly, stupid as stone,
But when it finally makes its way down the slope, over rocks

And weeds, through the razory grasses of the muddy shallows,
The water fanning out in loose circles around it
And then stilling, when it finally reaches the deepest spot

And raises in slow motion its perfectly articulated wings,
Wings of smoke, wings of air, then everything changes.
Out of the shallows the lovers emerge, sword and flame,

And over the pond's lone island the willow spills its canopy,
A shifting feast of gold and green, a spell of lethal beauty.
O bird of moonlight. O bird of wish. O sound rising

Like an echo from the water. Grief sound. Sound of the horn.
The same ghostly sound the deer makes when it runs
Through the woods at night, white lightning through the trees,

Through the coldest moments, when it feels as if the earth
Will never again grow warm, lover running toward lover,
The branches tearing back, the mouth and eyes wide,

The heart flying into the arms of the one that will kill her.

from *The Massachusetts Review*

Sonogram

◇ ◇ ◇

Something of desk work and pornography,
through succulences of conducting gel.
Vector: creation (in a partial view),

held in the half-dark of the examination room,
just as a wishbone of base mineral
holds pomegranate seed or emerald

or alveolus in a narthex rose.
God's image lies couched safe in blood and matter,
where an ionic snow falls lightly, hushed

into the deep calm of the body's gulf.
The channel-changer skates . . . tiny hot springs
of the beating heart, or sinuses of thought

like Siracusa's limestone quarries, where
an army of seven thousand starved to death.
The world of line and measure somewhat darkly

honors you in this glass, child: all your hands
will make, all your body will savor,
your mind consider, or your heart regret,

seeking your whole life for such immanence.

from *The New Republic*

CAROLYN KIZER

On a Line from Valéry

◇ ◇ ◇

Tout le ciel vert se meurt   Le dernier arbre brûle

The whole green sky is dying. The last tree flares
With a great burst of supernatural rose
Under a canopy of poisonous airs.

Could we imagine our return to prayers
To end in time before time's final throes,
The green sky dying as the last tree flares?

But we were young in judgement, old in years
Who could make peace; but it was war we chose,
To spread its canopy of poisoning airs.

Not all our children's pleas or women's fears
Could save us from this hell. And now, God knows
His whole green sky is dying as it flares.

Our crops of wheat have turned to fields of tares.
This dreadful century staggers to its close
As the sky dies for us, its poisoned heirs.

All rain was dust. Its granules were our tears.
Throats burst as universal winter rose
To kill the whole green sky, the last tree bare
Beneath its canopy of poisoned air.

from *Princeton University Library Chronicle*

1975

◇ ◇ ◇

Sodden on her bed,
we discussed rubato.
I zoned her crotch, deemed it
my focal point, my zero

degree: hetero coitus
was an engraved
manuscript whose figurations
I would trace

with an apprentice's slavish,
inauthentic brush.
Under the Blue Nun's influence
we smooched; a waxen

indifference, like hypothermia,
overtook me—also
a poignant intimation
that my intermezzo-loving

friend, in her sincere wish
to seduce me, had become
a suicidal emblem I could love,
her skin Fragonard

pink. She said, "If a guy is gay
there's a glaze
in his eyes. He looks
through you, doesn't see you."

Enlightened, I made a list
of possibilities
I planned, in dreams, to pursue:
the chef, the tuner,

the harpsichordist, the man
whose instrument I didn't know—
he seemed a clown, or acrobat.
I saw this carnival

curiosity in the laundry room.
He wore a muscle
shirt, black tights. His talk
was fast arpeggio, punctuated

by cackles. My whites
spun in the wash,
and then I moved them to the dryer,
after the saltimbanque

had removed his louche, aeolian linen.

from *Boulevard*

JOHN KOETHE

Falling Water

◇ ◇ ◇

I drove to Oak Park, took two tours,
And looked at some of the houses.
I took the long way back along the lake.
The place that I came home to—a cavernous
Apartment on the East Side of Milwaukee—
Seems basically a part of that tradition,
With the same admixture of expansion and restraint:
The space takes off, yet leaves behind a nagging
Feeling of confinement, with the disconcerting sense
That while the superficial conflicts got resolved,
The underlying tensions brought to equilibrium,
It isn't yet a place in which I feel that I can live.
Imagine someone reading. Contemplate a man
Oblivious to his settings, and then a distant person
Standing in an ordinary room, hemmed in by limitations,
Yet possessed by the illusion of an individual life
That blooms within its own mysterious enclosure,
In a solitary space in which the soul can breathe
And where the heart can stay—not by discovering it,
But by creating it, by giving it a self-sustaining
Atmosphere of depth, both in the architecture,
And in the unconstructed life that it contains.
In a late and very brief remark, Freud speculates
That space is the projection of a "psychic apparatus"
Which remains almost entirely oblivious to itself;
And Wright extols "that primitive sense of shelter"
Which can turn a house into a refuge from despair.
I wish that time could bring the future back again
And let me see things as they used to seem to me

117

Before I found myself alone, in an emancipated state—
Alone and free and filled with cares about tomorrow.
There used to be a logic in the way time passed
That made it flow directly towards an underlying state
Where all the minor, individual lives converged.
The moments borrowed their perceptions from the past
And bathed the future in a soft, familiar light
I remembered from home, and which has faded.
And the voices get supplanted by the rain,
The nights seem colder, and the angel in the mind
That used to sing to me beneath the wide suburban sky
Turns into dreamwork and dissolves into the air,
While in its place a kind of monument appears,
Magnificent in isolation, compromised by proximity
And standing in a small and singular expanse—
As though the years had been a pretext for reflection,
And my life had been a phase of disenchantment—
As the faces that I cherished gradually withdraw,
The reassuring settings slowly melt away,
And what remains is just the sense of getting older.
In a variation of the parable, the pure of heart
Descend into a kingdom that they never wanted
And refused to see. The homely notions of the good,
The quaint ideas of perfection swept away like
Adolescent fictions as the real forms of life
Deteriorate with manically increasing speed,
The kind man wakes into a quiet dream of shelter,
And the serenity it brings—not in reflection,
But in the paralyzing fear of being mistaken,
Of losing everything, of acquiescing in the
Obvious approach (the house shaped like a box;
The life that can't accommodate another's)—
As the heart shrinks down to tiny, local things.

Why can't the more expansive ecstasies come true?
I met you more than thirty years ago, in 1958,
In Mrs. Wolford's eighth-grade history class.
All moments weigh the same, and matter equally;
Yet those that time brings back create the fables
Of a happy or unsatisfying life, of minutes

Passing on the way to either peace or disappointment—
Like a paper calendar on which it's always autumn
And we're back in school again; or a hazy afternoon
Near the beginning of October, with the World Series
Playing quietly on the radio, and the windows open,
And the California sunlight filling up the room.
When I survey the mural stretched across the years
—Across my heart—I notice mostly small, neglected
Parts of no importance to the whole design, but which,
In their obscurity, seem more permanent and real.
I see the desks and auditorium, suffused with
Yellow light connoting earnestness and hope that
Still remains there, in a space pervaded by a
Soft and supple ache too deep to contemplate—
As though the future weren't real, and the present
Were amorphous, with nothing to hold on to,
And the past were there forever. And the art
That time inflicts upon its subjects can't
Eradicate the lines sketched out in childhood,
Which harden into shapes as it recedes.
I wish I knew a way of looking at the world
That didn't find it wanting, or of looking at my
Life that didn't always see a half-completed
Structure made of years and filled with images
And gestures emblematic of the past, like Gatsby's
Light, or Proust's imbalance on the stones.
I wish there were a place where I could stay
And leave the world alone—an enormous stadium
Where I could wander back and forth across a field
Replete with all the incidents and small details
That gave the days their textures, and that linked them
All together in a way that used to seem eternal.
We used to go to dances in my family's ancient
Cadillac, which blew up late one summer evening
Climbing up the hill outside Del Mar. And later
I can see us steaming off the cover of the Beatles'
Baby-butcher album at your house in Mission Bay;
And three years later listening to the Velvet
Underground performing in a roller-skating rink.
Years aren't texts, or anything like texts;

And yet I often think of 1968 that way, as though
That single year contained the rhythms of the rest,
As what began in hope and eagerness concluded in
Intractable confusion, as the wedding turned into a
Puzzling fiasco over poor John Godfrey's hair.
The parts were real, and yet the dense and living
Whole they once composed seems broken now, its
Voice reduced to disembodied terms that speak to me
More distantly each day, until the tangled years
Are finally drained of feeling, and collapse into a
Sequence of the places where we lived: your parents'
House in Kensington, and mine above the canyon;
Then the flat by Sears in Cambridge, where we
Moved when we got married, and the third floor
Of the house on Francis Avenue, near Harvard Square;
The big apartment in Milwaukee where we lived the
Year that John was born, and last of all the
House in Whitefish Bay, where you live now
And all those years came inexplicably undone
In mid-July. The sequence ended late last year.
Suppose we use a lifetime as a measure of the world
As it exists for one. Then half of mine has ended,
While the fragment which has recently come to be
Contains no vantage point from which to see it whole.
I think that people are the sum of their illusions,
That the cares that make them difficult to see
Are eased by distance, with their errors blending
In an intricate harmony, their truths abiding
In a subtle "spark" or psyche (each incomparable,
Yet each the same as all the others) and their
Disparate careers all joined together in a tangled
Moral vision whose intense, meandering design
Seems lightened by a pure simplicity of feeling,
As in grief, or in the pathos of a life
Cut off by loneliness, indifference or hate,
Because the most important thing is human happiness—
Not in the sense of private satisfactions, but of
Lives that realize themselves in ordinary terms
And with the quiet inconsistencies that make them real.
The whole transcends its tensions, like the intimate

Reflections on the day that came at evening, whose
Significance was usually overlooked, or misunderstood,
Because the facts were almost always unexceptional.
Two years ago we took our son to Paris. Last night
I picked him up and took him to a Lou Reed show,
And then took him home. I look at all the houses as I
Walk down Hackett Avenue to work. I teach my classes,
Visit friends, cook introspective meals for myself,
Yet in the end the minutes don't add up. What's lost
Is the perception of the world as something good
And held in common; as a place to be perfected
In the kinds of everyday divisions and encounters
That endowed it with integrity and structure,
And that merged its private moments with the past.
What broke it into pieces? What transformed the
Flaws that gave it feeling into objects of a deep and
Smoldering resentment—like coming home too early,
Or walking too far ahead of you on the rue Jacob?
I wish that life could be a window on the sun,
Instead of just this porch where I can stand and
Contemplate the wires that lace the parking lot
And feel it moving towards some unknown resolution.
The Guggenheim Museum just reopened. Tonight I
Watched a segment of the news on PBS—narrated by a
Woman we met years ago at Bob's—that showed how
Most of Wright's interior had been restored,
And how the ramp ascends in spirals towards the sky.
I like the houses better—they flow in all directions,
Merging with the scenery and embodying a milder,
More domestic notion of perfection, on a human scale
That doesn't overwhelm the life that it encloses.
Isn't there a way to feel at home within the
Confines of this bland, accommodating structure
Made of souvenirs and emblems, like the hammock
Hanging in the backyard of an undistinguished
Prairie School house in Whitefish Bay—the lineal,
Reduced descendant of the "Flameproof" Wright house
Just a block or two away from where I live now?
I usually walk along that street on Sunday,
Musing on how beautiful it seems, how aspects of it

Recapitulate the Oak Park house and studio, with
Open spaces buried in a labyrinthine interior,
And with the entrance half-concealed on the side—
A characteristic feature of his plans that made it
Difficult to find, although the hope was that in
Trying to get inside, the visitor's eye would come to
Linger over subtleties he might have failed to see—
In much the way that in the course of getting older,
And trying to reconstruct the paths that led me here,
I found myself pulled backwards through these old,
Uncertain passages, distracted by the details,
And meeting only barriers to understanding why the
Years unfolded as they did, and why my life
Turned out the way it has—like his signature
"Pathway of Discovery," with each diversion
Adding to the integrity of the whole.

There is this *sweep* life has that makes the
Accidents of time and place seem small.
Everything alters, and the personal concerns
That love could hold together for a little while
Decay, and then the world seems strange again,
And meaningless and free. I miss the primitive
Confusions, and the secret way things came to me
Each evening, and the pain. I still wonder
Where the tears went, standing in my room each day
And quietly inhabiting a calm, suspended state
Enveloped by the emptiness that scares and thrills me,
With the background noise cascading out of nothing
Like a song that makes the days go by, a song
Incorporating everything—not into what it says,
But simply in the way it touches me, a single
Image of dispersal, the inexhaustible perception
Of contingency and transience and isolation.
It brings them back to me. I have the inwardness
I think I must have wanted, and the quietude,
The solitary temper, and this space where I can
Linger with the silence curling all around me
Like the sound of pure passage, waiting here
Surrounded by the furniture, the books and lists

And all these other emblems of the floating world,
The prints of raindrops that begin as mist, that fall
Discreetly through the atmosphere, and disappear.
And then I feel them in the air, in a reserved,
More earthly music filled with voices reassembling
In a wellspring of remembrance, talking to me again,
And finding shelter in the same evasive movements
I can feel in my own life, cloaked in a quiet
Dignity that keeps away the dread of getting old,
And fading out of other people's consciousness,
And dying—with its deepest insecurities and fears
Concealed by their own protective colorations,
As the mind secretes its shell and calls it home.
It has the texture of an uncreated substance,
Hovering between the settings it had come to love
And some unformulated state I can't imagine—
Waiting for the telephone to ring, obsessed with
Ways to occupy these wide, unstructured hours,
And playing records by myself, and waking up alone.
All things are disparate, yet subject to the same
Intense, eradicating wills of time and personality,
Like waves demolishing the walls love seemed to build
Between our lives and emptiness, the certainty they
Seemed to have just two or three short years ago,
Before the anger spread its poison over everything.
I think about the way our visions locked together
In a nightmare play of nervousness and language,
Living day to day inside the concentrated
Force of that relentless argument, whose words
Swept over us in formless torrents of anxiety, two
People clinging to their versions of their lives
Almost like children—living out each other's
Intermittent fantasies, that fed upon themselves
As though infected by some vile, concentrated hatred;
Who then woke up and planned that evening's dinner.
It's all memories now, and distance. Miles away
The cat is sleeping on the driveway, John's in school,
And sunlight filters through a curtain in the kitchen.
Nothing really changes—the external world intrudes
And then withdraws, and then becomes continuous again.

123

I went downtown today and got a lamp with pendant
Lanterns made of opalescent art glass—part, I guess,
Of what this morning's paper called the "Wright craze."
I like the easy way the days go by, the parts of aging
That have come to seem familiar, and the uneventful
Calm that seems to settle on the house at night.
Each morning brings the mirror's reassuring face,
As though the years had left the same enduring person
Simplified and changed—no longer vaguely desperate,
No longer torn, yet still impatient with himself
And still restless; but drained of intricacy and rage,
Like a mild paradox—uninteresting in its own right,
Yet existing for the sake of something stranger.
Now and then our life comes over me, in brief,
Involuntary glimpses of that world that blossom
Unexpectedly, in fleeting moments of regret
That come before the ache, the pang that gathers
Sharply, like an indrawn breath—a strange and
Thoughtful kind of pain, as though a steel
Band had somehow snapped inside my heart.
I don't know. But what I do know is that
None of it is ever going to come to me again.
Why did I think a person only distantly like me
Might finally represent my life? What aspects
Of my attitudes, my cast of mind, my inconclusive
Way of tossing questions at the world had I
Supposed might realize another person's fantasies
And turn her into someone else—who gradually became
A separate part of me, and argued with the very
Words I would have used, and looked at me through
Eyes I'd looked at as though gazing at myself?
I guess we only realize ourselves in dreams,
Or in these self-reflexive reveries sustaining
All the charms that contemplation holds—until the
Long enchantment of the soul with what it sees
Is lifted, and it startles at a space alight with
Objects of its infantile gaze, like people in a mall.
I saw her just the other day. I felt a kind of
Comfort at her face, one tinctured with bemusement
At the strange and guarded person she'd become—

Attractive, vaguely friendly, brisk (*too brisk*),
But no one I could think might represent my life.
Why did I even *try* to see myself in what's outside?
The strangeness pushes it away, propels the vision
Back upon itself, into these regions filled with
Shapes that I can wander through but never see,
As though their image were inherently unreal.
The houses on a street, the quiet backyard shade,
The rooms restored to life with bric-a-brac—
I started by revisiting these things, then slowly
Reconceiving them as forms of loss made visible
That balanced sympathy and space inside an
Abstract edifice combining reaches of the past
With all these speculations, all this artful
Preening of the heart. I sit here at my desk,
Perplexed and puzzled, teasing out a tangled
Skein of years we wove together, and trying to
Combine the fragments of those years into a poem.
Who cares if life—if someone's actual life—is
Finally insignificant and small? There's still a
Splendor in the way it flowers once and fades
And leaves a carapace behind. There isn't time to
Linger over why it happened, or attempt to make its
Mystery come to life again and last, like someone
Still embracing the confused perceptions of himself
Embedded in the past, as though eternity lay there—
For heaven's a delusion, and eternity is in the details,
And this tiny, insubstantial life is all there is.
—And that would be enough, but for the reoccurring
Dreams I often have of you. Sometimes at night
The banished unrealities return, as though a room
Suffused with light and poetry took shape around me.
Pictures line the walls. It's early summer.
Somewhere in *Remembrance of Things Past*, Marcel,
Reflecting on his years with "Albertine"—with X—
Suggests that love is just the consciousness of distance,
Of the separation of two lives in time and space.
I think the same estrangement's mirrored in each life,
In how it seems both adequate and incomplete—part
Day-to-day existence, part imaginary construct

Beckoning at night, and sighing through my dreams
Like some disconsolate chimera, or the subject
Of a lonely, terrifying sadness; or the isolation
Of a quiet winter evening, when the house feels empty,
And silence intervenes. But in the wonderful
Enclosure opening in my heart, I seem to recognize
Our voices lilting in the yard, inflected by the
Rhythms of a song whose words are seamless
And whose lines are neverending. I can almost
See the contours of your face, and sense the
Presence of the trees, and reimagine all of us
Together in a deep, abiding happiness, as if the
Three of us inhabited a fragile, made-up world
That seemed to be so permanent, so real.
I have this fantasy: It's early in the evening.
You and I are sitting in the backyard, talking.
Friends arrive, then drinks and dinner, conversation . . .

The lovely summer twilight lasts forever . . .

                                        What's the use?
What purpose do these speculations serve? What
Mild enchantments do these meditations leave?
They're just the murmurs of an age, of middle age,
That help to pass the time that they retrieve
Before subsiding, leaving everything unchanged.
Each of us at times has felt the future fade,
Or seen the compass of his life diminished,
Or realized some tangible illusion was unreal.
Driving down to Evanston last week, I suddenly
Remembered driving down that road eight years ago,
So caught up in some story I'd just finished
That I'd missed the way the countryside was changing—
How in place of trees there now were office towers
And theme parks, parts of a confusing panoply of
Barns and discount malls transfiguring a landscape
Filled with high, receding clouds, and rows of flimsy
Houses in what used to be a field. I thought of
Other people's lives, and how impossible it seemed
To grasp them on the model of my own—as little

Mirrors of infinity—or sense their forms of
Happiness, or in their minor personal upheavals
Feel the sweep of time reduced to human scale
And see its abstract argument made visible.
I thought of overarching dreams of plenitude—
How life lacks shape until it's given one by love,
And how each soul is both a kingdom in itself
And part of some incorporating whole that
Feels and has a face and lets it live forever.
All of these seemed true, and canceled one another,
Leaving just the feeling of an unseen presence
Tracing out the contours of a world erased,
Like music tracing out the contours of the mind—
For life has the form of a winding curve in space,
And in its wake the human figure disappears.
Look at our surroundings—where a previous age
Could visualize a landscape we see borders,
Yet I think the underlying vision is the same:
A person positing a world that he can see
And can't contain, and vexed by other people.
Everything is possible; some of it seemed real,
Or nearly real, yet in the end it spoke to me alone,
In phrases echoing the isolation of a meager
Ledge above a waterfall, or rolling across a vast,
Expanding plain on which there's always room,
But only room for one. It starts and ends
Inside an ordinary room, while in the interim
Brimming with illusions, filled with commonplace
Delights that make the days go by, with simple
Arguments and fears, and with the nervous
Inkling of some vague, utopian conceit
Transforming both the landscape and our lives,
Until we look around and find ourselves at home,
But in a wholly different world. And even those
Catastrophes that seemed to alter everything
Seem fleeting, grounded in a natural order
All of us are subject to, and ought to celebrate.
—Yet *why*? That things are temporary doesn't
Render them unreal, unworthy of regretting.
It's not as though the past had never happened:

All those years were real, and their loss was real,
And it *is* sad—I don't know what else to call it.
I'm glad that both of us seem happy. Yet what
Troubles me is just the way what used to be a world
Turned out, in retrospect, to be a state of mind,
And no more tangible than that. And now it's gone,
And in its place I find the image of a process
Of inexorable decay, or of some great unraveling
That drags the houses forward into emptiness
And backwards into pictures of the intervening days
Love pieced together out of nothing. And I'm
Certain that this austere vision finally is true,
And yet it strikes me as too meager to believe.
It comes from much too high above the world,
And seems to me too hopeless, too extreme—
But then I found myself one winter afternoon
Remembering a quiet morning in a classroom
And inventing everything again, in ordinary
Terms that seemed to comprehend a childish
Dream of love, and then the loss of love,
And all the intricate years between.

from *Western Humanities Review*

Troubling the Water

◇ ◇ ◇

As if that night
  on Fire Island
    never happened—the dune

buggy that cut
  like a scythe of moonlight
    across the sand—I see

Frank O'Hara
  with Mapplethorpe's
    book of photographs.

He whistles "Lover
  Man" beneath his breath,
    nudging that fearful

40th year into the background,
  behind those white waves
    of sand. A quick

lunch at Moriarty's
  with someone called LeRoi,
    one of the sixty best friends

in the city. He's hurting
  to weigh Melville's concept
    of evil against Henry

James. That woman begging
a nickel has multiplied
a hundredfold since

he last walked past the House
of Seagram. They speak
of Miles Davis

clubbed twelve times
outside Birdland by a cop,
& Frank flips through pages

of Mapplethorpe as if searching
for something to illustrate
the cop's real fear.

A dog for the exotic—
is this what he meant?
The word Nubian

takes me to monuments
in Upper Egypt, not
the "kiss of birds

at the end of the penis"
singing in the heart
of America. Julie Harris

merges with images of Bob Love
till *East of Eden* is
a compendium of light

& dark. Is this O'Hara's
Negritude? The phallic temple
throbs like someone

breathing on calla lilies
to open them: Leda's
room of startled mouths.

from *Urbanus*

Getting the Message

◇ ◇ ◇

God, the rabbis tell us, never assigns
exalted office to a man until
He has tested his mettle in small things.
So it is written in the *Midrash*
that when a lamb escaped the flock Moses
overtook it at a brook drinking its fill
and said, I would have taken thee in my arms
and carried thee thither had I known thy thirst
whereupon a Heavenly Voice warmly
resounded, *As thou livest, thou art fit.*

Divine election's scary. The burning bush
might have been brightened by St. Elmo's fire
according to *The Interpreter's One-Volume
Commentary*. The slopes of Exodus,
scrub growth close-cropped by tough horned herds
of Jacob's sheep (now prized as an heirloom breed)
lack treetops, mountain peaks or spires
that might discharge electrical ghost-plumes.
St. Elmo's seems less science than the desire
of modern exegetes to damp the flame.

I like my Bible tales, like Scotch, straight up
incontrovertible as Dante's trip
through seven circles, Milton's map
of Paradise or Homer's wine-dark epic.
On such a stage there falls a scrim between
text and critique where burst of light may crack
and dance as if on masts of sailing ships

and heavenly voices leap from alp to plain.
In Sunday School I shivered at God's command:
Take off thy shoes, thou stand'st on holy ground

and lay awake in the hot clutch of faith
yearning yet fearful that the Lord might speak
to me in my bed or naked in my bath.
I didn't know how little risk I ran
of being asked to set my people free
from fording some metaphorical Red Sea
with a new-sprung Pharaoh raging at my back.
I didn't know the patriarchy that spared me
fame had named me chattel, handmaiden.
God's Angels looked me over but flew by.

I like to think God's talent scouts today
select for covenant without regard
for gender, reinterpreting The Word
so that holy detectives glossing the bush
(most likely wild acacia), scholars of J
E and P deciphering Exodus
will fruitfully research the several ways
divine authentication lights up truth.
Fragments of it, cryptic, fugitive
still spark the synapses that let us live.

from *Tikkun*

Bridget

◇ ◇ ◇

As I remember, I was that kind of girl. I was
Like Bridget, I read about her in the *Plain Dealer*,
Who was shot in the arm because her brother wanted
To live with his mother. "We'll kill ourselves if we don't
Get to," they dared the SWAT team, and the team killed
Their friend Jason. The entire telephone transcript
Started on the front page, it was lengthy, many shots
Were fired, and Jason died for the sake of strength,
He found out he had none, he flew into a rage
Because a cop tossed a pack of cigarettes, bought
To calm him, onto the deck instead of into his hand;
He fired at the cop, he missed, no cops were killed.
Then they blasted a hole in his neck. That was
The way Bridget described it, sobbing into the phone,
"My friend has a hole in his neck." Her brother said,
"My partner has a gap in his mouth." Bridget said,
"There's blood sticking out." She's fourteen.
She was shot in the arm. She was standing behind Jason.
She told the police she had to be there for her brother
Wanting to live with their mother. I was like that.
I got in trouble because of boys. I tagged along
When they committed crimes, I held their dope, they said
There was no way I'd be searched but it wasn't true,
The cops were smarter and the cops were mean,
They figured out a way. The cops told Jason
He wasn't in trouble so he wouldn't shoot himself.
He called them fuckers. They told Brian he wasn't
In trouble, then arrested him. That's what Jason said

They'd do, for once he was right. It's not the law
Not to lie to kids. There are good reasons to lie
To kids, if they're hurting themselves, or they might
Hurt others; that's what cops say. Maybe they're right.
But cops made me take off my clothes for them;
And they were in uniform.

I was like Bridget. I wanted to do right by boys.
Sometimes they'd smile in my direction, showing
Bad teeth that proved they were country; sometimes
They promised they'd take care of me. I don't know
What happened the night I went to jail. I stared down
The angles of the blue-strobed field, we'd had a wreck
By a pasture, there were cops, there were parents,
I mean my mother and stepfather, it was a small town,
A southern small town, and I went to jail at seventeen
To keep the boys from going. Bridget was shot.
She'll never recover. I never did. I feel like you,
Bridget, but now I know better, I wish you did;
I like to say I never knew my father. You must've
Been living with yours. I know how it feels
To take too long to figure it out: they don't want us,
Bridget, we're a fuck to them, that's how we got here
And how they'd touch us if the law allowed; it does,
They fucked us good. Nothing makes us feel
Ourselves like a fuck we've felt before, if it's father,
A cold hard fuck, if it's mother, a wet sloppy fuck,
If it's brother, short and quick like a ferret's tongue,
Like the feet of the hamster racing his wheel
Every night while we dream of men; if we wake up
We'll begin to fear them. Now in my dream I hear
The voice of your brother calling 911, I dream
The shapes of his features screwed up as he cries,
"The cops just shot my partner," and "Somebody come
Please help my partner." I dream the question
Of the sides of the law. Bridget, we have to hide ourselves,
Because we can't help it, we want to help, and it always
Seems right, there are men on each side, sometimes
They extend a hand looking able to hold much more

Than ours, their voices are saying, "Come to me, come,
Only here I'll protect you," and you don't say no
To a smile like that. You rush to kneel by the fallen
Friend, wet teeth shining through a gap in his head.

from *American Poetry Review*

My Night with Philip Larkin

◇ ◇ ◇

Rendezvous with dweeby Philip in the shower:
"Aubade" taped up on pale blue tile;
I can hear him grumbling through the falling water.
Uncurling steam is scented with a trace of bile,
And I'm as grateful as a thankless child can be.
Someone has been here in this night with me,
Someone whose bitterness, I want to say,
Is even more impressive than my own.
Talking with Larkin on the great white telephone
I let the night be washed out into day

Until it's safe enough to go lie down
And dream of my librarian, my bride.
Perhaps he sits and watches in his dressing gown;
I know he won't be coming to my side
For fumblings and words he simply can't get out.
That stuff was never what it was about
When he would wake at four o'clock to piss
And part the curtains, let the moon go on
With all the things worth doing, and not done,
The things that others do instead of this.

from *B City*

Refuge

◊ ◊ ◊

When the shooting started, he crawled under
a loose board into some kind of animal shed.
Little room to move, even less light—a smell
of dried sweat and shit in the rickety walls.
They had swung around the corner, Jeep-mounted
machine guns, swerving so hard the firing
seemed accidental, the gunners untrained
or drunk, hanging on wildly while one Jeep
fishtailed and the other went up on two wheels.
But the bullets ran neatly up the street
to a whitewashed wall where graffiti artists
had worked, like cat burglars, after curfew;
a woman carrying a big tin of milk in front
of one misspelled slogan tripped over
a puff of dust; everyone dove and slid.

Something made a throaty noise in one corner
of the shed. Shit, he thought, a dog, a mean pig.
Pulling one foot back for a good kick he flicked
his lighter: two girls gasped at his big shoe.
They had shiny clutch-purses, eyeshadow and rouge
like bruises. Knees drawn up, they were naked
under vinyl miniskirts. They tried to hide
in each other's hair. Snapping the lighter shut,
he tried to reconstruct what minutes ago
had been a tourist stroll: goat and pig heads
hung outside a market stall, a barefoot man
in ripped shorts and top hat hawked brass bells

to scare away demons. The peanut vendor bent
over an oil-drum oven, his sash of peanuts
rattled with street-corner authority.
Store and house fronts leaned flaky pastel walls
against each other, four boys squatting
in the gutter pounded roll caps with brick.
He'd set his camera for automatic exposure.
Much later he saw it hadn't been loaded.

The shooting was blocks past the shed now.
He was sick of animal shit and darkness
and girl-whores pissing terror in the straw.
OK, he thought, you send bullets running up
somebody's steps to pound the door, break it down
and find who it is you want, because bullets
do it faster, bullets don't waste time on coffee
and dirty jokes or get shot serving a warrant.
He saw the logic—move fast, hit hard,
get the fuck out. But he let the whores crawl out
first. The click of their spike heels vanished
unchallenged across the street. Emerging himself,
he saw the peanut vendor's sash in the road.
The postcard pastels of houses and stores were pimpled
with bullet holes. A boy's bare legs stuck up
feet first from a storm drain. One of the feet,
as he watched, began to relax and bend back,
slowly as a dancer's foot, toward the ground.

He was walking fast, trying to slap the smell
of dung-straw off his shirt when something slipped
around his ankle, almost tripped him. A hand,
a woman's hand—the milkwoman who got caught
by the wall. Lying in a dusty whitish puddle,
she had a hole in her chest: sucking in wheezes,
blowing out red bubbles. He started to kneel,
but he didn't want to get stopped with the camera
and hard currency. He had to focus on the hand
—not the wound, not the face. Starting on the little
finger, he worked it loose, then the ring finger,

and so on. Holding the hand open and away
from his leg, he wadded some bills into it
and pressed it shut before trotting off again.
Enough for a doctor maybe, he guessed, but if not
—he was running now—enough for a decent burial.

from *Manoa*

J A M E S   L O N G E N B A C H

What You Find in the Woods

◇   ◇   ◇

Nothing in the air to call me here—
The trees recede into the dark circumference
Of the hill, and everything's reduced
To the chilled circle of its lesser self.
No muddy spoor, no red sleeve of a fox
Against the snow. But things accumulate
As if from nothing: nests of broken glass;
A frozen mess of feathers, kicked, upturns
The bird intact, the tiny beak a rictus.

As a child, I lived near woods like these
And followed older boys who'd stumbled
On a child's body, wrapped in wool—nothing
Left but sinew tangled with the bones.
What's this? The bark of sycamores that's flaked
Away like skin. Trees shift uneasily—
A hawk, its wings too lofty for this wood,
Descends to look at me; its head turns once
Before the branch it straddles breaks away.

Then nothing. Silence thinning on a hill
Too low for speculation on our lives—
There's nothing here I don't already know.
So more than anything, more than the slow,
Determined beat of wings, I'm on the lookout

For the bone, the skeleton half buried
In the leaves, the body sprinkled hastily
With dirt and sticks, the open hand, the plain
Disheveled face no stranger than my own.

from *The Yale Review*

Fracture Santa Monica

◊ ◊ ◊

Don't walk like a drunken sailor,
my trainer scolds, as I lope across Ocean
Avenue, dreamscape of my lopsided autumn.

Odd men and women swathed in blankets applaud
when I place the broken left foot in front
of the okay right, then reverse without a hitch

and walk backwards, toward the pier,
the polluted Pacific. Why, they're applauding
my ligaments, my courage! The way I back into

traffic, the traffic signal's bird-cheeps
saving my life! They rise from their bedrolls
of stains and infirmity and the clapping

dies. *Heel, toe! heel, toe! heel, toe!*
I back through the detritus, the eucalyptus,
the Cirque du Soleil spinning behind me.

What's to be glad about or proud of
when the smallest dire injury begins
my downhill glide to self-pity, to hyperboles

of despair? I'm a parvenu, a cat-scratch
in this seascape of amputations, I'm
selfish, selfish, the trainer snaps,

What are you good for, dragging in the sand?
Who's it gonna help if you fix that foot?

from *Colorado Review*

My Mammogram

◇ ◇ ◇

I.

In the shower, at the shaving mirror or beach,
For years I'd led . . . the unexamined life?
When all along and so easily within reach
(Closer even than the nonexistent wife)

Lay the trouble—naturally enough
Lurking in a useless, overlooked
Mass of fat and old newspaper stuff
About matters I regularly mistook

As a horror story for the opposite sex,
Nothing to do with what at my downtown gym
Are furtively ogled as The Guy's Pecs.

But one side is swollen, the too tender skin
Discolored. So the doctor orders an X-
Ray, and nervously frowns at my nervous grin.

II.

Mammography's on the basement floor.
The nurse has an executioner's gentle eyes.
I start to unbutton my shirt. She shuts the door.
Fifty, male, already embarrassed by the size

Of my "breasts," I'm told to put the left one
Up on a smudged, cold, Plexiglas shelf,
Part of a robot half menacing, half glum,
Like a three-dimensional model of the Freudian self.

Angles are calculated. The computer beeps.
Saucers close on a flatness further compressed.
There's an ache near the heart neither dull nor sharp.

The room gets lethal. Casually the nurse retreats
Behind her shield. Anxiety as blithely suggests
I joke about a snapshot for my Christmas card.

III.

"No sign of cancer," the radiologist swans
In to say—with just a hint in his tone
That he's done me a personal favor—whereupon
His look darkens. "But what these pictures show . . .

Here, look, you'll notice the gland on the left's
Enlarged. See?" I see an aerial shot
Of Iraq, and nod. "We'll need further tests,
Of course, but I'd bet that what *you've* got

Is a liver problem. Trouble with your estrogen
Levels. It's time, my friend, to take stock.
It happens more often than you'd think to men."

Reeling from its millionth Scotch on the rocks,
In other words, my liver's sensed the end.
Why does it come as something less than a shock?

IV.

The end of life as I've known it, that is to say—
Testosterone sported like a power tie,
The matching set of drives and dreads that may
Now soon be plumped to whatever new designs

My apparently resentful, androgynous
Inner life has on me. Blind seer?
The Bearded Lady in some provincial circus?
Something that others both desire and fear.

Still, doesn't everyone *long* to be changed,
Transformed to, no matter, a higher or lower state,
To know the leathery D-Day hero's strange

Detachment, the queen bee's dreamy loll?
Oh, but the future each of us blankly awaits
Was long ago written on the genetic wall.

V.

So suppose the breasts fill out until I look
Like my own mother . . . ready to nurse a son,
A version of myself, the infant understood
In the end as the way my own death had come.

Or will I in a decade be back here again,
The diagnosis this time not freakish but fatal?
The changes in one's later years all tend,
Until the last one, toward the farcical,

Each of us slowly turned into something that hurts,
Someone we no longer recognize.
If soul is the final shape I shall assume,

(—*A knock at the door. Time to button my shirt*
And head back out into the waiting room.)
Which of my bodies will have been the best disguise?

from *Poetry*

HEATHER McHUGH

And What Do You Get

◇　◇　◇

Excise the er from exercise. Or from
example, take the ex out: now it's bigger;
to be lonely, take the amp out
and replace it with an *i*. Take am or me
away from name
and suddenly there's not
much left, the name's one of the many names

for naught. Eleven tons of hidden work
are always lurking inside words. In English or
analysis (the cons turned pro, among the -fessions)
take in out
of mind and you've

got someone who delivers you a bill.
Take double you from anybody's will—
a skew, a skid—and all
is terrifying—
take the *the* from

therapist, split accent with an id—

from *Urbanus*

Exchange of Fire

◇　◇　◇

When your left arm touched my right
as we both reached for the dessert
menu in the all-night diner, a spark
began smoldering in my sleeve, broke
a hole the size of a heart in the patched
elbow of your jacket.

Dirty white smoke enveloped our bodies
as the conversation turned
to the underground fire we'd all seen
on the news, a fire that had raged up
to consume everything in its path.
The air in the diner stank of charred meat;
under the table I took my husband's right
hand and placed it on my left thigh
where flesh and garter meet.

I wanted only that, until your left knee
grazed my right, and this time
there was an explosion, just as our waiter
lit the crêpes Suzette your wife had ordered
for you. Flames engulfed our table
and we moved to another booth, my husband
and your wife saying *we can't take*
you two anywhere simultaneously.

I had to decide: should I risk
asking for something sweet now, or abstain?—
when you said think of the women on the *Titanic*

who pushed away from dessert that night
because their skirts were getting tight.
It made me think all right

and then when we were all friends again,
laughing, the whole length of your left leg
rubbed the length of my right and every
light in the joint went out, life stopped
for me, it meant a scandal somewhere in the future.

I tried to focus on the scorched dessert
menu feeling the beginnings of violent
pleasure. I reached for my knee where the hair
had been singed off, where the flesh was
already oozing, and I remember thinking,
I like this. It was the beginning
of loneliness, also.

For when the lights came back on I was
afraid to move from my seat; when we rose
to say good night we would be expected
to embrace. We had to: the flesh

of your body down the length of my trembling
body, the thin cloth covering my breasts
covered with flames, the apologies to your wife
for the plastic buttons on your shirt front melting,
your belt buckle welding us together in our heat.

At home I'm still burning when my husband
pours lighter fluid on his hands and feet and sets
himself on fire: only by entering fire can I
put the fire out. This time I might finally
do it. It may be a threat, an end to pain,
or all there is left to make of love.

from *Nimrod*

Shooting for Line

◇ ◇ ◇

for Bob Hershon

To break the silence or your newly acquired Ming vase,
or raise my expectations and the flag over the Brooklyn Navy
  Yard.
To employ a veritable army of secretaries, or your for once
  awake faculties
in coming to grips with the enemy, the notion that nothing
  outlasts our fleeting perception of it
in addition to reflecting on the newly painted wall and what
  just transpired,
slurred speech and the passage from the Schumann
permitting some liberties, the picnic to go on as originally
  scheduled.

If you paint the garage door green, yourself into a corner
(to stagger home at midnight, the times people come and go from
  work)
it may be to place objects in the memory, the lips on the hard
  rubber mouthpiece
before turning the room upside down, a deep scarlet.
Meanwhile changing to life-support or funky black-tie
is a far cry from poisoning the drinks or good names
of those who fly Cessnas or the banners of dubious political
  loyalty
in the name of something higher or Benedict Arnold,
or cutting to the chase, an armful of her favorite wildflowers.
And yet the fall is precipitous, warmer than in any of the six
  preceding years.

To rewrite the book on how to be obnoxious in public and
    Stéphane Mallarmé.
Once you are involved in the institutional end of the arts and her
    lustrous hair,
it isn't to pinpoint excess, the exact spot where the light
    appears to transcend itself.
It is possible to run in circles or a decent-sized refrigerator
    business
without diffusing all of your energies, a greenish blue ink
    through ordinary tap water,
or paying out bonuses every Christmastime, the fishing line over
    the rippling pond . . .
I mean, to count your real blessings, how many stars make up the
    Little Dipper;
open the door to the shed or an account at the local bank
so that attention can be paid, the overdue electric bill.

Whoso list to hunt and the names in the beat-up address book
I know better, contract law in the state of Idaho.
To respond to the veiled plea or unusual stimuli
carries with it an obligation to be human, a satchel containing
    the proceeds for that week
serving a dual purpose and all who may have been kept waiting
as a result of the traffic controllers' strike, a hopefully
    temporary abandonment of the notion of quality.

To lap the ailing runner or the dish of milk,
bask in Florida sun and her praise,
coming to New Jersey on Jan. 16, innumerable times like a hot
    pan of popcorn.

Still to consider changing jobs or popular fiction in light of
    the new and highly suggestive deconstructive techniques.
Who doesn't seek to improve basic reading skills or the land,
write off a fair-weather friend or a sequel to *War and Peace*?
It isn't rehashing the past, yesterday's shepherd's pie,
to blow the whistle on the funeral industry, the wet shutters
    seemingly all night long—
to endow her with more than the eye can see, a small liberal
    arts college

to the tune of $300 million and "Hail to the Chief"
touching most major side issues and the place where scar tissue
   had substantially healed,
or ruling the letterhead paper and what is in reality an
   extremely small fiefdom
to hit the nail on the head, a "frozen rope."
To divide your love equally or anything but a prime number,
lose your balance or your index cards;
or single you out from all others, through the drawn-in infield

while moving heaven and earth, the carefully crated stemware.
It opens new doors, the season of mists
and mellow fruitfulness. Pen the hogs; your last will and
   testament
relating to the issue under advisement, your mother's side:
to catch the meaning and/or Walter Johnson
colored by unconscious associations and the barely discernible
   tints of February's
trial balloon by long-forgotten ordeal.

In short, we hold certain truths to be self-evident but the
   answers in code in the glove compartment,
and they eat up the presumed distance and the leftovers
like an unenacted crime bill or Sophocles' *Oedipus at Colonus.*
It seems likely that no one leaves *all* hope behind, a calling
   card
fringed in tears and a raised border
but the wounds are bathed in salt, also the cocker spaniel.
It is taking not prisoners but a glass of red wine,
prendre un verre mais aucun prisonniers
bei mir bist du schön but you also block out the reading light
in which an axe is being sharpened, my appetite for new
   experience

making up for lost time and ghost stories to tell to the kids
   on Halloween.
The truck rolled up the kilometers, down the steep incline.
Sometimes taming a wild horse or an uncontrollable urge
can lead to unlooked for results, a battalion into a no-win
   situation

proving the guilt of those accused, particularly flimsy.
Wake up the sleeping giant, those planning to leave bright
    and early before breakfast,
or fly in the face of conventional wisdom 500 miles north to
    Saskatchewan
for the solution to appear, sun through dense fog
dispersing warmth and shadows of telephone poles
as habits die hard, hornets sprayed with Raid.
It used to be filling an Angora sweater and a rackety DeSoto
to shadow your memories and the branch-haunted garage door,
what used to be called hope, or Brenda,
leaving aside questions of good taste and muddy shoes
to make for the hideout concealed behind dense shrubbery, a
    potentially dangerous enemy.
So it meant pulling the plug on candor and the black-and-white
    t.v. set.
I'm warming up to you, the macaroni and cheese in the toaster
    oven.
All in all, I find myself elbowing the impatient tourist and
    incipient greed
out of the way, Bed o' Roses by Man o' War,
while they skate mostly on thin ice, the plans and those with
    rented blades,
time borrowed and old Benny Goodman records,
rounding things off to the nearest 100 and the corner on two
    wheels

to snap up the latest hit, you out of your pool of lethargy.
Meanwhile to compete with your cheekbones and a phantom
the sun burns fair skin and sometimes bridges,
let me not sing doo-wop or the raptures of never knowing
    enough about you;
or if new opportunities spring up and occasionally wild dogs
it pays to look managerial, the runner back to first base.
In light of winter and your extreme position
it seems best to avoid rhyme, entanglements of all kinds.
How many gloomy outlooks or peeling sills are painted
to reveal the inevitable, a view of barges in the Hudson
without assigning all of Hart Crane and their real property
and thus realigning priorities and tires grown threadbare

like the solution to a nonexistent puzzle, sodium chloride
    in a liter of Scotch,
so that the temptation to take a drink, provide a quick fix,
takes a back seat to language, the mature driver?

Gather up ye goatherd gods and your wits
which have fallen on the gym floor, our distinctly hard times.
When the sun sinks its nail into the boards of earth

the approach is cloudy, by way of the town dump.
Put out the cat, and then put out the cat.
Then it fell out, hair and what was portended,
that some trusted to luck, the self-styled family advisor
bestowing largesse of a kind and the kids on the grandparents
    for the entire weekend.
How to play the Barber piano sonata or the tricky futures market
without driving yourself crazy, 12 hours without stopping,
speaking volumes and the "degree" speech from *Troilus and
    Cressida*?
For you can break the bank or its dark green shaded windows,
attack inefficiency or an undefended knight
while spending more than you earn in a year, your semen like Don
    Juan.
This is keeping the tempo honest, an herb garden out of the shadow
    of the air conditioner,
farming rocky soil and half the copyediting
to avoid stress-related illness of all kinds or an onrushing
    locomotive;
or take Ibuprofen tablets every 4 hours plus the not so subtle
    hint
to correct the condition as well as each major sentence error
to move the greatest number of readers, the computer table over
    near the window
shaded by a thin curtain and the deepening afternoon.
If the answer falls on deaf ears or short of satisfying,
it only serves the lowest common denominator, a tennis ball right
    over the wire fence,
dying on the vine, or in your arms
as Keats proposed to do and Fanny Brawne,
remembering the Alamo and the toothpaste.

To conclude: rooted in good loamy soil and the Lockean doctrine
   of individual rights,
firing the old flintlock and the watchman,
shooting for line or at the absolute outside the middle of next
   March.
If you push your luck or the dangerous passed pawn all the way
   to the eighth rank
it may help to collect items from the suggestion box, your wits
   where they still lie,
effectively closing the book and the prolonged meeting.
It amounts to the same: larding lectures with factitiously
   appealing anecdotal material
or the beef with fat despite consequences to the arteries.
Or you can put your stamp on the postcard or postmodern American
   poetry
or motion to the auctioneer for an adjournment
to lend an air of April and your very best blue suit:
sweep the minefield clear and all the accumulated dust into the
   corner.

from *Hanging Loose*

GEOFFREY O'BRIEN

The Interior Prisoner

◇ ◇ ◇

A translation of an unsigned manuscript
written at Salamanca around 1902

1.

They search out new regions of muteness.

The sounds the wind makes
as it rips among the hollows

they organize into a dialect.

Always where they have found nothing
they place a stone to mark the spot.

2.

If a shaft of light broke into a thousand pieces
and each piece into a thousand more,
might not a stranger
mistake any of the fragments for the original light?

Am I not such a stranger,
and if so
how can I speak of light or its origins?

What I have taken for light
may be something entirely different:
blood, or mire, or darkness itself.

3.

The spider's purity of intent,
the radiance of the design
its appetite makes.

4.

There was a king who commanded his subjects
to rebel against him,
upon penalty of death whether they obeyed or refused.

5.

Gold. A decayed residue of light.
Bog creatures swarm to its glow.

In the phosphorescent dusk
they feed on the sun's excrement.

6.

The tongue has made a name for itself,
and seeks to declare independence from the mouth.

7.

A lexicon contains words as a prison contains men.
At most I make the prisoners merry enough
to forget their chains for an hour.
What sentence would free them?

8.

The light advancing across the face of the wall . . .
A discovery of the Indies,
enacted each morning like clockwork.

9.

Their need
—to drink, to quarrel, to display—
is not so much their sickness as their wealth.

They cannot endure the poverty of being without desire.
No more can I,
needing as I do my emptiness and loss of appetite.

10.

There is a fountain
lulled by its splashing
and recirculating waters

into so deep a sleep
it forgets it's a fountain.

In the heart of that sleep it dreams of a fountain.

11.

A prophet covered in blood,
a baby howling warnings
in the dead of winter

to frightened ignorant villagers
who stifle its cries
for fear of murderous soldiers.

That is what they call Christmas.

12.

The saints turn life inside out
so that the death side shows.

They expose death to ordinary daylight,
as if in life they were already a head on a platter
or a body shot full of arrows.

This provokes horror and amazement among the onlookers,
whose first instinct is to side with the Roman soldiery
and exterminate the monsters.

13.

Being is a mouth
with which an unknowable word articulates itself

in a language which is the partial imprint
of something prior to speech,

like the impression left in grass
where an animal has rested.

14.

The pilgrim retraced his steps
to the point where he went astray
and found no path or hole.

This barricaded thicket
was indeed his native country.

On that spot
he built a shrine
to the patron saint of desertion.

15.

Our history begins
with the description of an injury
whose particulars were never before written down.

The wound does not heal
but from now on it can never be forgotten.

We have made a language
sacred to the memory of pain.

16.

Not even as many notes
as would make a song,

not even as many syllables
as would make a name.

Just enough air
to make a breath:

that is the prairie, the kingdom,
the boundless estate.

17.

Day wasn't long enough
for more than a few words:

nerve, cobweb,
fracture, lichen, bud,

the goat's anxiety,
the telescope

the previous tenant left behind.
Whatever else was said

got torn apart
when the rain drove through.

from *Hambone*

JACQUELINE OSHEROW

Late Night Tête-à-Tête with a Moon in Transit

◇ ◇ ◇

Che fai, tu, luna, in ciel, dimmi, che fai,
Silenziósa luna?

I've always wished that I could ask that question,
Though I'm not one to ask that sort of thing
And I'd probably spoil it in translation;

Besides, the moon won't tell me what it's doing,
Caught, like a wayward kite, up in that tree,
And reaching for a cloud's extended wing . . . .

But I'd still love to float some words above me
To palm stray silver or maybe panhandle
The leaves' new-minted coins from that flush tree.

Usually I write these things to people,
But why not, since no one else is listening,
Address myself to you, *luna in ciel,*

Who have left the tree, the cloud, are no doubt hastening
To strain the face of some unknowing city
With your own relentless questioning.

Do you remember that time in Newark, when you took pity
On the semi-burnt-out towers at the city's rim?
Maybe it was just a show of vanity,

That you make things of beauty even of them
And their misshapen friends, the cast-iron bridge
And pock-marked stretch of road that hauled me home:

Sudden adornments on an orange, huge,
Dome-shaped temple rising from the ground
To which a desperate skyline had made pilgrimage,

Its high-rises prostrate on the holy ground,
Like throngs in Mecca, hearing their muezzin.
And there was Newark, momentarily crowned—

As if by that ecstatic, praying din—
For once in its stunted life, with gold, not thorns,
A colossal halo where its sky had been,

Seeming to say that when a city burns
It doesn't actually have to be consumed.
I suppose, if there's a God, these are His concerns,

But you'd know better than I; it's you He named,
On the fourth day, by name, and there you were.
You still arrive as if you'd just been dreamed

Out of nothing by a reckless dreamer's dreamer,
Or, rather, out of nothing but a word.
Did you hear it called or was it all a blur—

The stars' wild glittering, a fish, a bird,
Howling animals, a man, a woman
And, before you'd settled in, their young son murdered . . .

I wonder if you caught a glimpse of sun
Before you had to go your separate ways.
Perhaps, in all this time, you've never known

About the routine epochs we call days
When a good deal less of what we are is hidden.
You're off wandering in a foreign maze

Of branches, wires and rooftops, until a sudden
Undoing of the darkness sends you back to us.
But I've seen you, in the daytime, come unbidden,

As if you preferred to be anonymous,
A tiny, unassuming moon-shaped cloud
Half trying to hide, half to spy on us.

Perhaps that's what you were doing in Leningrad
When I took a walk at dusk along the Nevsky Prospekt
And caught you setting up a masquerade

As one of the heavy globes that intersect
The once grand boulevard at every step,
Lighting the way for palaces, absurdly decked—

Like stout, old matrons in a bridal shop—
In frilly and unflattering pastels.
You hovered over them as if to eavesdrop

As they murmured to their doubles in canals,
Your deadpan face unnaturally low
And white light clinging to their scarred pastels

Until they seemed to fill with early snow.
You were still there when I entered my hotel
But you must've risen eventually; you had to

Once you'd heard what they were willing to tell.
Maybe they recited a local poem
In which the Neva casts her murky spell,

A great one, maybe, like the *Requiem*
Extorted from the woman in gray-blue shards of paint
Who presides over the Russian Art Museum

Along with several icons of a Russian saint—
Nicholas, maybe?—and a lone Chagall.
She—though I'd never read her—managed to haunt

My travels just by staring from that wall.
Now I'd scour the city for some mirage
Of her, in the House on the Fontanka, at her table

Coaxing warring ghosts onto a page
From their flimsy strongholds in the air.
In those days, all I cared for was the Hermitage:

Simone Martini's Mary, bent to hear,
But cut away from her announcing angel,
Deep blue robes engulfing all of her

(Their color, egg whites crushed with lapis lazuli)
To frame each long white hand's elaborate wing
And the features streaming down her twisted, frail

Face intent, exquisitely, on nothing.
I saw her counterpart in Washington years later:
An all-gold angel, tiny, glittering,

Also Simone Martini, also pure,
Olive branch in hand, hailing the wall,
His message reaching to the North Atlantic somewhere

To be salvaged by a pious, passing sea gull
Who flew to Leningrad, as if on pilgrimage,
And circled the museum screaming, *Hail*

Unless he was trying, moon, to pay *you* homage—
With his faith he could see you in the daytime
Despite your elaborate camouflage—

Or maybe to the huge Matisses in the museum,
So bright they grabbed his keen eye through the windows.
Is that what *you* were doing, moon? Staring at them:

The lavish dining room, the couple in pajamas,
Palm fronds on Morocco's stucco domes,
And next to a squatting outdoor orchestra's

Scraggly band, with knees and hands for drums:
That iron-pumping remake of *La Danse*,
Inspired, doubtless, by the high, taut limbs

Of the Ballets Russes' still unmatched Nijinsky
Who'd stay limber for an endless quarter century
At the window of his dull asylum in France

Listening for the wind to stir a tree
With a long legato like the solo moan
That slithered down, then up, the flute that Debussy

Commissioned to awake his sleeping faun.
Who knows what Anastasia would wait
For at the window of *her* asylum—French? Italian?

She remembered nothing, not the heavy velvet
Her mother made her wear that so encumbered
Her entrance to the royal box, in state,

Where her father, when it darkened, always slumbered
As her mother shed her jewels and ermine cape.
If Anastasia had heard that flute, she'd have remembered

Nijinsky's stunning grand finale leap,
Anything beside the string of closed, dark spaces
That constituted her pyrrhic escape.

I wonder if she ever saw those huge Matisses,
If Nijinsky saw his likeness in *The Dance*,
If they would have even known each other's faces

If they'd been in the same asylum, in France.
Perhaps they were, already, too much changed—
It wouldn't really have been a great coincidence,

A place known to Russians, who arranged
With a jewel or two, the care for noble émigrés—
Only Matisse's painting is still unchanged:

The exploding torsos, limbs, necks, fingers, toes.
I just saw it hanging in New York,
At least as graceful as it ever was.

That's right, if unbelievable: New York.
Along with all its cronies (well, not all;
They decided—though its picture's in the book—

That *La Musique* was too infirm to travel).
But the people in pajamas, the green Moroccan,
That dining room with roses on its wall,

Were there with several prostrate, white-robed men,
Each of whom resembled a praying dome.
And I'd thought I'd never see those paintings again,

Had sacrificed all Leningrad to see them,
Staying from nine in the morning until dark
Or dusk, rather, in each resplendent room.

But there they all were, hanging in New York.
You were there, too, posing as a water tank
Atop one of the towers that line the park

And then as a new ornament for Citibank.
You'll forgive me, won't you, if I wasn't fooled?
I *was* glad to see you there, absurdist, blank,

Holding your milky own against the cold.
Why should Matisse be more footloose than you?
And why should I have felt so ridiculed

That what I'd made a pilgrimage to know
Had come, of its accord, a dozen years later?
How could anyone have guessed that now

Leningrad would again be named for Peter?
Not the saint as much as the young czar,
Who, posing as a sailor on a freighter,

Found one thing in all the world to long for:
A cluster of islands in a slim lagoon—
Have you ever been there? I've not seen you there,

Though I can't say I was looking for you, moon—
That had spent so long refining their reflection,
Trying first these towers, then these arches, on,

This jagged bridge, this square, this predilection
For a line of marble porticoes, a dome,
That Peter, almost instantly, began construction

Of a copycat version, nearer home,
Where the Neva's ice would copy it again . . .
How his architects must have longed for Rome

Or wherever they'd come from, Florence, Naples, Milan,
Lured by who knows how much Russian gold
And the wild ambition—madness?—of the plan

To clear some empty marshlands near a sea and build
Of all things, a northern rival to Venice.
The first foundations shattered in the cold

Or floundered in the swamp and mud and ice;
Thousands upon thousands of workers died.
Of what? Drowning? Frostbite? Typhus? Tetanus?

I looked it up, in the encyclopedia, under Leningrad,
And found out Peter never made it to Venice.
He was on his way, but stopped, the entry said,

Because of a rebellion—at home? in Venice?
Who was it who rebelled? Could they have won?
And what could Peter have seen that would entice

Such single-minded purpose from a person?
A Canaletto? An engraving? Was it just the legend?
Maybe he saw his city in a vision;

It didn't resemble Venice in the end.
Not, of course, that any city could,
Though it is, in its clunky way, certainly grand.

But why am I telling you? You've surely made
An occasional impression on the Grand Canal
Or slipped it silver from behind a cloud

Where you'd set up your temporary arsenal.
But Venice has no need for your loose change
Or for your services as would-be sentinel.

It's one place your white light can't unhinge
Though you might put a word in with the tide
To slow each palace's unconscious plunge

Into the Adriatic's murky bed . . .
Imagine those canals reflecting only clouds
Like mirrors in a house of mourning, covered.

I ought to have learned by now that each thing fades,
Probably, almost all without a trace.
Why should a place like Venice beat the odds

When we haven't got one relic from Atlantis?
You could probably describe the place in detail,
The pools where you'd admire your still-young face,

The pillars you'd turn nearly blue, the wall
Where a sculpted hero mourned the child-apprentice
Who took himself too near the sun and fell

Into the waiting sea, just like Atlantis
And, soon, now, Venice and the other city-myths
Whose names alone could at one time entice

A thousand dreaming princes to their deaths
As they surveyed building sites for ideal plans,
Scoured continents for masons, sculptors, goldsmiths,

Glaziers, painters, marble, tiny stones,
To fill ten thousand ceilings with mosaics,
Not a glint of one of which remains.

But aren't you also made of rocks?
Not a wanderer, after all, but a place,
Devoid of even the crudest human tricks.

And your enchantress's serene, pearl face
Is actually nothing more than a reflection.
So whom am I talking to? And what does this

Make me, but a reflection of a reflection,
These lines a sort of verbal hall of mirrors,
Paling copies of copies in each direction

Of the copied plans of czars, doges, emperors,
Not one of them accurate or thorough,
But variants on whimsies, envies, errors,

Something like my long obsession with you;
I, too, would love to alter every city
With my own flawless arsenal of silver-blue

And ignore the pressing accidents of gravity,
Or at least seem to, as you've always done,
And burn whatever's dreary, banal, petty

With a subtle glitter borrowed from a sun
No one on their piece of earth can see.
I'd have a worthwhile answer to your question

If, by some fluke, you should one day call to me—
What's up, loquacious person, what are you doing?—
As you rest against a local cloud or tree,

My face transfixed and overflowing
With so much white and silver that the jealous stars
Would leave their constellations and come following—

The sky a mess of limbless lions and bears
Stranded centaurs, hunters, wingless swans—
Until they'd rearranged themselves as dancers,

Deposed Russian princesses, lost fauns,
Rebels, painters, architects, pretenders
To a restless century's discarded thrones,

All of them waiting, breathless, at their windows
For even the most diminished kinds of signs
Except for those few enterprising wanderers

Who scavenge local shores for telltale stones
And could be said, in all their travels, to mimic you.
Perhaps, among them, there are some lucky ones

Who find some rocks from which they can construe
A wall or tower or bridge or an entire town
And then there are those who simply wait for you

To come to them and tell what you have seen.
I know for a fact you've obliged some of them;
With Akhmatova you had a nightly conversation

And with Peter, disappointed, on his voyage home.
He was lucky, really, not to have seen San Marco;
This way, he was satisfied with one gold dome

And a brick palace covered in yellow stucco.
Perhaps it was you who suggested it,
You, who sent Matisse off to Morocco—

So Petersburg is lovely only by your light
And, as a symbol on a mosque, at least,
Matisse was finally forced to paint your portrait.

Poor old moon, I suppose you couldn't resist
You, too, have suffered great indignities—
Men trampling on you, shuttles roaring past,

Bits of you in all our major cities,
The night-time sky clogged with man-made rivals.
You, whose likenesses had once been deities,

With sacrifices nightly, temples, festivals,
Now, on some nights, make your rounds as modestly
As a retired civil servant on her travels.

But, still, couldn't you tell me what you see?
I've waited so long, and fairly patiently
Che fai, tu, luna, in ciel? Dimmi

from *Western Humanities Review*

MOLLY PEACOCK

Have You Ever Faked an Orgasm?

◇ ◇ ◇

MY COLLEGE SEX GROUP

All my girlfriends were talking about sex
and the vibrators they ordered from "Eve's
Garden" which came with genital portraits
of twelve different girls. All my friends' needs
swirled around me while their conversations
about positions crescendoed and they waved
their vibrators—black rubber things. Saved
by volubility I looked at the relations
of labia to clitorides—look, there was one
like mine, labia like chicken wattles
below a hooded clitoris. "Friends!
of these twelve genital portraits, which
are you?" I couldn't ask them. Happy
to have found a picture of one like me:
the portrait held the hair all back and popped
the clitoris out like a snapdragon
above the dark vaginal stem.
Oh God, it was me! (and another, I stopped,
there were others like us, throughout the world).
When my order for the vibrator was filled,
I'd get my own portrait. I'd show it to the next boy
before I got undressed, "Here's what you're getting."
And I'm not alone, or ugly, if that's what you're thinking.

175

THE RETURN

When I open my legs to let you seek,
seek inside me, seeking more, I think
"What are you looking for?" and feel it will
be hid from me, whatever it is, still,
or rapidly moving beyond my frequency.
Then I declare you a mystery
and stop myself from moving and hold still
until you can find your orgasm. Peak
is partly what you look for, and the brink
you love to come to and return to must
be part of it, too, thrust, build, the trust
that brings me, surprised, to a brink of my own . . .
I must be blind to something of my own
you recognize and look for. A diamond
speaks in a way through its beams, though it's dumb
to the brilliance it refracts. A gem at the back
of my cave must tell you, "Yes, you can go back."

THE RULE

Completely naked, mons completely gray,
my mother tells me how to masturbate
leaning over the couch where down I lay
in my dream. But I know how! You're too late!
Too often we have to wait for our guides.
Completely naked, mons completely brown,
will I invite her to lie down, who prides
herself on never touching, let alone
holding, stroking, licking? I don't,
though if I wait perhaps she will come of
her own powers, and then we will make love.
Will we be guilty, taking our love loaned
from a dream? Or will curiosity
free us from "Be Still," and let us be?

Have You Ever Faked an Orgasm

When I get nervous, it's so hard not to.
When I'm expected to come in something
other than my ordinary way, to
take pleasure in the new way, lost, not knowing

how to drive it back to sureness . . . where are
the thousand thousand flowers I always pass?
the violet flannel, then the sharpness?
I can't, I can't . . . extinguish the star

in a burst. It goes on glowing. Your head
between my legs so long. Do you really
want to be there? I whimper as though . . . silly . . .
then get mad. I could smash your valiant head.

"You didn't come, did you?" Naturally, you know.
Although I try to lie, the truth escapes me
almost like an orgasm itself. Then the "No"
that should crack a world, but doesn't, slips free.

I Consider the Possibility

Long waisted, tender skinned and, despite the gym,
love roll about the midriff above the leggy limbs
muscled into knots at each calf, "beautiful for your age,"
—bend over naked from your waist and show your red half
peach of cunt to me who has fumbled at my cage
trying key after key in the stuck door with a half laugh
after each failure, let me lay the bone of my nose
on the peach flesh and lift up my mouth to the pit
as I reach my arms toward the inverted throes
of your breasts, and as I touch your orange nipple tips
know that I have striven all my life toward men
and now, marriageless again, gossiping with my mother
who bluntly suggests that there are always women
and upon being merrily teased by my therapist
at the prospect of our love affair (thinking that "the other"

has never incited such laughter), let me touch your wrist
at the dinner table, and begin the silly maneuver
that will lead me to hold your head, to smooth your
hair all back, as going through keys at the door my own wrist
finally turns tender side up as the lock untwists.

from *The Paris Review*

Toys

◊ ◊ ◊

Seeing them like this,
arranged according to size,
sectioned off by color,

I think it's not so much their being
made mostly for men, nor anything in
their being man-made; it's what

they are made *of*, disturbs me: rubber
and urethane, plastic aiming for
the plastic of flesh,

and just missing. Growing up, I was
told once that, somewhere in the Vatican,
there's a room still, where—

ordered and numbered, as if
awaiting recall—lie all the phalluses
of stone, granite, tufa, fine marble,

that were removed from pagan statues
for lacking what any leaf, it seems,
can provide: some decorum.

I've never seen them, but their beauty,
I imagine, is twofold: what they're
made of, for one—what, in cracking,

suggests more than just the body that
came first, but the peril,
the vulnerability

that is all the flesh means to say,
singing; then, what even these
imitations before me—lesser somehow

but, to the eye and to touch, finally
more accurate, in being true
to an absurdity that is always there

in the real thing—even these seem
like wanting to tell about beauty,
that it also comes this way, in parts.

from *Boston Phoenix*

MARIE PONSOT

Old Mama Saturday

("Saturday's Child Must Work for a Living")

◇ ◇ ◇

"I'm moving from Grief Street.
Taxes are high here
though the mortgage's cheap.

The house is well-built.
With stuff to protect, that
mattered to me,
the security.

These things that I mind,
you know, aren't mine.
I mind minding them.
They weigh on my mind.

I don't mind them well.
I haven't got the knack
of kindly minding.
I say Take them back
but you never do.

When I throw them out
it may frighten you
and maybe me too.

        Maybe
it will empty me
too emptily

and keep me here
asleep, at sea
under the guilt quilt,
under the you tree."

from *Western Humanities Review*

How Light Is Spent

◇ ◇ ◇

Two half-brothers fully blind living together
a historian and a piano player. Neither
cared for birds, cacophonous carriers of lice,
birds. Both uncles blind from birth.

                    Half my uncles' days
no darker than any child's sleep but the sounds
that came, their one talent listening, through
thin walls were death to hide:

                              distraction being
the better part of valor after spring
thaw the forsythia bend graceful above
pools admiring their own linear progression.

The vanity of the blind manifests
in a soul more bent to serve to present
its true account—or returning the soul
returning like a vampire in the morning
to darkness after the dark

                              day labor light
denied. The two blind uncles
would walk with new girl friends in the spring park
down prim paths patient to prevent the murmurs
but children would giggle like tinfoil as they passed
children would glitter hysterical

as they kissed.
Bearing the mildest yoke of a little lust
blind uncles walked home to an apartment shared
like kingly state. Spring birds blared
from skies but blind uncles passed them by.

Thousands speed
without rest but two blind uncles for dinner
stand caressing peas on a plate at three o'clock,
mashed potatoes at nine, the plate a clock face,
a form of knowledge like sight. Before bed then
to stare through any wall

at this dark world and
wide. And the reading of bedtime stories
the outdoing of one's self undoing partial
life a knotted ball of yarn ambitious to be
a sweater. The felt life. The history
of the dark is the music of sleep.

from *Pequod*

How Late Desire Looks

◇   ◇   ◇

To begin with something not already caught
In the current of another's life, an indifferent
Hand of transparent wind playing first
With the sleeve at your damp wrist, then
Pressing strands of hair sideways against my
Mouth, the beautiful coming, like a gift
Of the rare indigo bunting, body turquoise
At your feeder in the slanting light, soft
Particles of air, silting through high aspens
To settle around us like hope itself. I could

Watch you carry a clear glass jar of water
Walking nowhere in particular, at least
Forever—back and forth across your yard
Where five orange poppies, like saucers
Tilt together on slender necks, and scents
Of globe basil, nicotiana and lilies intermix
Because you've cultivated this rocky, sloping
Piece of wilderness into a place to live—
Just for the way what looks in your eyes
Like thirst, holds me contained one minute

Longer than intended, since I'm a neighbor
Merely returning a borrowed bicycle or book
And even now we hear your wife's car grind
Into the drive, arriving, and the startled
Bunting, which is actually black but for a
Complex pattern of diffraction through its
Structure of feathers, suddenly takes off

So that what remains are a few chickadees,
The most common yellowthroat, taunting:
Which-is-it, Which-is-it, Which-is-it
And the grosbeak with its rose-breasted blush.

from *Harvard Magazine*

MICHAEL J. ROSEN

The Night Before His Parents'
First Trip to Europe
His Mother Writes a Letter
"To Our Children"

◊   ◊   ◊

On the envelope, her lone instruction
is boldface, all caps: **DO NOT OPEN**.
He pictures, inside, the slanting hand that bore him
their news each week that he lived overseas.

And yet beyond a list of policies,
securities and keys, the words his mother
confessed she agonized over the eve of departure
are yet unutterable as joint untimely deaths.

This scene of composition, so inexplicable—
his mother, sleepless at the kitchen table
addressing her children from the other side
of tragedy, then phoning, "I'd be too embarrassed

if you read it; I'm no writer like you"—
this scene obscures what work the son has done.
As if, in that unlikely event, his grief
would want a poem from her! Words to critique,

revise into some pretense of posterity!
If only his own work could seal such feeling
in an envelope someone might hold, hold dear
and never open, exposing its words to light.

Two weeks, the letter rests on the unset
table, holding his parents' place in the house
until their return, when the letter disappears,
replaced by snapshots stamped *Oct 90*.

These the children share around the table,
proving their parents had gone, at last, to Europe,
happier at fifty-nine and sixty-one
than they can remember. Next trip—their dates

are set, the planes and time-shares, booked—
they will be farther, longer, and no safer,
leaving behind that or a different letter
to route the rest of our untravelled lives.

from *Salmagundi*

KAY RYAN

Outsider Art

◇　◇　◇

Most of it's too dreary
or too cherry red.
If it's a chair, it's
covered with things
the savior said
or should have said—
dense admonishments
in nail polish
too small to be read.
If it's a picture,
the frame is either
burnt matches glued together
or a regular frame painted over
to extend the picture. There never
seems to be a surface equal
to the needs of these people.
Their purpose wraps
around the backs of things
and under arms;
they gouge and hatch
and glue on charms
till likable materials—
apple crates and canning funnels—
lose their rural ease. We are not
pleased the way we thought
we would be pleased.

from *Partisan Review*

The Age of Reason

◇ ◇ ◇

"When can we have *cake*?" she wants to know.
And patiently we explain: when dinner's finished.
Someone wants seconds; and wouldn't she like to try,
while she's waiting, a healthful lettuce leaf?
    The birthday girl can't hide her grief—

worse, everybody laughs. That makes her sink
two rabbity, gapped teeth, acquired this year,
into a quivering lip, which puts an end
to tears but not the tedium she'll take
    in life before she's given cake:

"When I turned seven, now," her grandpa says,
"the priest told me I'd reached the age of reason.
That means you're old enough to tell what's right
from wrong. Make decisions on your own."
    Her big eyes brighten. "So you mean

I can decide to open presents first?"
Laughter again (she joins it) as the reward
of devil's food is brought in on a tray.
"You know why we were taught that?" asks my father.
    "No." I light a candle, then another

in a chain. "—So we wouldn't burn in Hell."
A balloon pops in the other room; distracted,
she innocently misses talk of nuns'
severities I never knew at seven.
    By then, we were Unitarian

and marched off weekly, dutifully, to hear
nothing in particular. "Ready!"
I call, and we huddle close to sing
something akin, you'd have to say, to prayer.
   Good God, her hair—

one beribboned pigtail has swung low
as she leans to trade the year in for a wish;
before she blows it out, the camera's flash
captures a mother's hand, all hope, no blame,
   saving her from the flame.

       from *The Threepenny Review*

Transit Authority

◇ ◇ ◇

The journey is never what's expected.
  But we persist. Something goes wrong
on the other side of the tattered freeway
  so that the traffic is backed up for miles.
Someone gets out of his car to stare ahead
  with a hand shielding his eyes from the
   sun
the way the sailors once did sighting land,
  only his frown hints he may be on
   empty.

Minutes from now he could be scrambling
  through an opening in the hurricane fence
or walking with a can down the on-ramp
  where some drivers now escape in
   reverse.
We're lucky the road spreads out before us
  like a clear runway, but we're not
   satisfied.
It's as if the odometer is stuck on the nines,
  the infernal ticking of the last digit won't
   stop.

Gradually, the familiar skyline looms ahead
  gently coated with the smoggy haze of
   dusk,
in sharp contrast to the assortment of cars
  that have been picked to the bone and
   burned

appearing periodically in the breakdown lane,
    like profane doodles in the margin of a
      Bible
you just happen to pick up in a motel room,
    the ones that smudge if you try to erase
      them.

Were we meant to travel at such speed?
    Is it only a sensation that things pass us
      by,
as if televised, as if programmed for us,
    a myriad of façades inevitably giving way
to sudden vistas where we get a glimpse
    of the industrial water gleaming in the
      distance,
soon to be interrupted by a row of windows,
    some containing figures we can't quite
      make out?

Experience turns into a handful of change
    dropped again and again into the metal
      basket
so that the gate goes up and we move on,
    well aware that at this juncture the road
      narrows
and we become part of the same intensity
    others feel even when they roll up their
      windows
and proceed with the tentative resolve
    of angels approaching earth for the first
      time.

from *The Yale Review*

STEPHEN SANDY

Threads

◇ ◇ ◇

BOLTS

The logs of wool jersey plastered with labels
Lay in the lint and litter, columns in a heap
Like a Doric temple left at the shipping dock,
Trucked in from Dan River.
                                   They smelled so sweet,
Concentric rings like cross sections of a tree;
But these would shrink, unwound on the cutting block
Long as an alley to the boy who wheeled them in.
Whistling finale, faille unrolled on the table's
Spotlit runway, layer on layer, flat
For the cutter's saw following paper template
To carve out panels of dresses, thirty deep.
   That trade, like subsistence farming through thick and thin;
The rounds of seasons, this year's style or that
Year's loss; core sample of eternity.

1945

Ribbed faille sings out when it unrolls across
Itself; bolt after bolt lay up, unite
For the blade of Izzy, like a doctor dressed in white,
Sleeves starchly rolled up burly arms; the hum
And glitter of the little circular knife
Softly screaming through reds and tawny umbers
And a sheaf of special orders, orchid and plum;

Glazed taffeta slides, but wool packs tight like moss
For the muscular fist gripping the steel. Rosa,
Testy assistant, baleful refugee,
Helps Izzy—and only Yiddish between them. She
Must keep one sleeve rolled over the indigo
Tattoo; but after work would show its numbers,
Inky brand of her undeniable life.

SHIPPING BOY

Bald Applebaum of Shipping sampling lunch,
Your Virgil and your boss down those dark aisles,
From his wire cage—riffling through order files
With a licked finger—barked: forget it, the Punch
And Judy!—whatever looked too good to him
He called *the Punch & Judy*. Crocodile's
Tears, that was her *Shtick*; and then the smiles!
It was all *chutzpah*, Rosa playing it so grim.
He stirred his soup with awful satisfaction,
Stirring with pride or failure—hoping to score
From the dark of the back office—warned: she taunts
You; she's a designer; you are the attraction;
The boss's boy better get over it before
She bares you her arm and gets just what she wants.

LUNCHBOX

Tin lunchbox open, she smokes and watches out
The eighth-floor window. Pigeon; sky; one cloud.
Watches her forearm and sees nothing but—
Nothing. Dull parchment of untanned skin.
What morning music is this place about
She wonders, as the distance they've allowed
Her grows in this limbo where the door is shut
On the living; for now is for the dead, for kin,
For smoke and looking down at odors, where sweet-
Smelling threads and swags of lint coax a cough.

The numbers do not float away like dust,
Lint dust that swirls with operators' sweat
Billowing from machines someone turns off;
These strange "girls," how innocent and robust.

from *The Paris Review*

The Present Perfect

◇　◇　◇

I saw the cells on tv, as they swam
up to the egg, tails lashing, and I heard
the wind-tunnel sound they make, the steady hum

of thousands, blind, threadlike, worn, but soaring
through waterfalls in their drive to live, move,
and set the egg revolving like a star.

For us, there was no miracle of birth.
No genes, no geniuses. And yet, OK,
we had other things: our work, our history

scrawled on Margaux labels and libretti,
and, after all, no cribs, no sticky plums,
no pulling paper napkins, one by one,

from a metal box, to mop up dumped ice cream.
But then again, no immortality:
in my religion, children to speak my name

after I am. No heir to your kindness,
your skill with a kite, your father's whimsy,
or to my mother's mother's diamond pin.

And yet, we had each other's silences;
freedom to wander with no fixed plan,
now fixed in photos of sylphs that resemble us,

peering down cliffs in Brittany at ragged boards
floated up from dinghies lost at sea,
searching for fish carved into chapels' altars,

spending our suns like out-of-date coins,
until we reached the present-perfect tense—
that have-been state where past and future merge:

We have been married thirty-four years.
I see the kids we were frisk on this lawn
in the late afternoon's unnameable light.

Too late for them, and for their unborn kids,
but not too late for us, here among cedars,
to praise the fires in rose petals on slate;

white rhododendrons, a fountain's rainbow.
I see the dot of you, meadows away,
that grows in sight as you pedal home;

your reddish hair and beard, now tarnished silver,
that once we wanted for a chromosome;
your silhouette in a Manet-like straw hat

as you bless your new astilbe: "Live and be well,"
casting aside your customary questions
for an irrational faith the plant will grow;

I hear your voice that calls me to see wildflowers
poking through gravel cracks in our neighbors' driveway,
slender but fortunate, built to last their day.

from *Boulevard*

Avec Amour

◇ ◇ ◇

There never was a war that was inward.
MARIANNE MOORE

1

The first time I entered France, not by storm
but in a storm, I was met by uniformed

gendarmes with anxious-looking M-16s
shouldered on baby-faced intensity—

the same look I wore on my own young face—
my life, too, was a loaded gun, misplaced.

This was Paris in the sober eighties.
I'd come by boat from Dover in what we

at home call a nor'easter, to Calais,
shipwrecked hair in a Channel-knotted braid,

my Levi's salted stiff with water, my books:
on Vita's and Violet's sisterhood,

another on female orgasms, were
soaked to twice their size, swollen metaphors.

2

Soaked through like a swollen metaphor,
I'd come with someone I don't remember.

I no longer know her name or her hopes
but we kept each other company on the boat,

then the train, in the dismal, droning rain,
and in the gray room where we were detained

by overeager customs inspectors
who frisked me, my duffel bag, and guitar

case. In case of what? Hash? I didn't know
French, and what's worse, there were traces of smoke:

twigs, seeds, papers. They were after weapons
I wasn't carrying, but would have been

had it been the forties, and they Vichy.
I'd have been a Jew with an M-16.

3

I felt like a Jew without her M-16.
After hours (years) of hard questioning,

we were freed and the ardent rain stopped screaming.
We checked into a pension run by

a thin man and his even thinner wife.
Bolted in like refugees, by nine they'd locked up tight.

I was running from Steve, whom I'd left behind
at Kennedy. Really, it had been he

who had long before abandoned me.
Then, I hid. He had male lovers by thirteen.

He'd say he had to do family errands,
but by dinner he'd come around again

with hickies his mother thought came from me.
With the purple marks he also brought a twenty.

4

With the purple marks he brought a twenty
we'd spend on a dime bag and Burger King.

He didn't eat. Instead he got up a dozen times
for mustard, ketchup, ice, another drink.

Licking the salt off the damp, limp fries,
my briny predicament crystallized.

He'd been blowing johns in Fort Lauderdale.
I reasoned that impersonal sex paid well.

Thirsty from the salt, tired of sex talk,
we made out in his van, but always stopped

short, his half-cocked cock sheltered in his pants,
my crotch disarmed by my lack of interest.

The twenty spent, the rendezvous could end.
We tired of picking names for unborn children.

5

Give the imaginary name, Diane,
to my quiet, straight traveling companion.

Give her the understanding she lacked when
she realized that I'd gone to find the kind

of company she wasn't interested
in. We lasted two nights in the same bed.

When she figured out who I was, she left.
I wondered what I had said, then didn't,

then rode down the Boulevard St. Germain
where women glided down the avenue, arms

around each other's waists or hand in hand.
I thought I had died and gone to heaven,

not realizing what I'd seen was simply fashion.
Touching meant much more, or less, where I'd been.

6

Touching meant much more, or less, where I'd been.
But on the bus I thought I felt something

touch my backside. I thought it was an armrest,
an umbrella, grocery sacks that were set

in the aisle. Convinced it was harmless—
a bottle of lemon or orange citrus,

a roast, baguette, a protruding fennel—
I rode with the small pain and I smiled.

Two stops later he grabbed my breasts,
as he released my ass from his five-mile grasp.

I looked around for help that didn't come,
and said one of the French words I knew: *cochon*!

I read in bed through the rest of the trip
and the next time I entered France equipped.

Equipped, in love, two Jews with valid documents,
both post-Stonewall smart, one generation apart.

Only one, it turned out, had been liberated.
We loved, we laughed, we couldn't make it

last. I couldn't commit in French or English.
Instead, we lasted as passionate correspondents

who wrote through the recent maelstrom that cost you
your right breast. (The one I kissed when I kissed you.)

Now you and I fight this last late-century war—
not with language, self-censorship or pride,

Nazis, each other, or anti-Semites—
but against cells gone to tumors, gone to knives.

I enter France in a mnemonic storm tonight.
Never, though, to lose you a second time.

from *The American Voice*

ALAN SHAPIRO

Manufacturing

◇ ◇ ◇

Up in the billboard, over old South Station,
the Captain, all wide grin and ruddy cheek,
held up a golden shot of Cutty Sark
high as the skyline where the sunset spread
a gold fan from the twig-like spars and rigging
of a departing clipper ship. Above
the picture the dull haze of a real sun rose,
dragging the day up with it. Seven o'clock.
The agitated horns, brakes, fingers and catcalls
down below me were already merging
and channeling everybody on to warehouse,
factory, department store and office.

My father and uncle talking over all the goods
to be received that day, the goods delivered,
their two reflections in the window floating
like blurry ghosts within the Captain's grin,
their voices raised a little above the soft
erratic humming of the big machines,
the riveters and pressers, warming, rousing:
The Century order, did it get out last night?
And had the buckles come from Personal?
Who'd go do Jaffey? Who'd diddle Abramowitz
and Saperstein? Those cocksucking sons of bitches,
cut their balls off if they fuck with us. . . .

How automatically at any provocation
I can aim the words at anybody now,
woman or man, the reverberating angry

this, not that, in "pussy," "cocksucker,"
"fuckhead," hammered down so far inside me
it's almost too securely there to feel.
But I was thirteen then, and for the first
time old enough to have my father say
these things in front of me, which must have
            meant
I was man now too, I listened (blushing,
ashamed of blushing) for clues of what it was
I had become, or was supposed to be:

It did and didn't have to do with bodies,
being a man, it wasn't fixed in bodies,
but somehow passed between them, going to
by being taken from, ever departing,
ever arriving, unstoppable as money,
and moving in a limited supply
it seemed to follow where the money went.
Being a man was something that you did
to other men, which meant a woman was
what other men became when you would do
            them.
Either you gave a fucking, or you took one,
did or were done to, it was simple as that.

Somebody shouted from beyond the office
that Tony had passed out in the can again.
The lush, the no good lush, my uncle said,
get him the fuck out of here for good, will ya.
The stall door swung back, scrawled with giant
            cocks,
tits, asses and cunts, beyond which in the shadows
my father was gently wrestling with the man,
trying to hold him steady while his free hand
shimmied the tangled shorts and trousers up
over the knees and hips, and even got
the shirt tucked in, the pants zipped deftly enough
for Tony not to notice, though he did.

Even then I knew they'd fire him,
and that it wasn't gratitude at all
that made the man weep inconsolably,
his head bowed, nodding, as my father led him
to the elevator, still with his arm around him,
patting his shoulder, easing him through the door.
I knew the tenderness that somewhere else
could possibly have been a lover's or a father's
could here be only an efficient way
to minimize the trouble. And yet it seemed
somehow my father was too adept at it,
too skillful, not to feel it in some way.

And feeling it not to need to pull back,
to separate himself from what the rest
of him was doing, which was why, I think,
his face throughout was blank, expressionless,
like the faces of the presidents on the bills
he handed Tony as the door slid shut.
The men fast at the riveters and pressers
and the long row of women at the Singers
were oil now even more than men or women,
mute oil in the loud revving of the place,
a blur of hands on automatic pilot,
slipping the leather through the pumping needles,

under the thrusting rods, the furious hammers,
the nearly invisible whirring of the blades.
Come on now, Al, it's time, my father said,
and the Captain seemed to grin a little wider,
as if his pleasure there at the end of his
unending day grew freer, more disencumbered,
because he saw me at the start of mine,
under my father's arm, his soft voice broken
against the noise into an unfollowable tune

of favors and petty cash, and how much ass
he had to kiss to get me this, and I
should be a man now and not disappoint him.

from *TriQuarterly*

Brotherhood

◇　◇　◇

Deep in the nightmare of narrative, narrating
the nightmare, he is the author of this misery
dispossessed. He wonders how he should stand
at the public shore where sand and liquid salt
immerse immobile feet as if it still were summer,
as if the soothing brine weren't tainted
by the trash tugs plying the horizon.
He wants to know how to turn back, get on the bus
and pay the fare; how to allow the head to drift
against the window towards the scenic reverie
pavements repossess (a sheltered suburb
shaded with plane trees), and not
drift into thoughtless sleep. He'd like to steal
his life back, hour by per-hour-wage, he'd like to rewrite
the working week. Each word means so much
if just properly placed. Can he bring the sentence
to a satisfying close, begin the new phrase? He's a hero
of helpless questioning. (Quizzical virtue.)
The beach dusted with milky stars on Sunday
evenings, breakwaters built against the hurricanes
that battered banks all through his schoolbook
civic histories, have become an exercise
in self-composure before the eight o'clock alarm.
He tries immortalizing the mirage in hasty notebooks
on the train to work, the clauses broken

by the bell that means his stop. He stops, begins,
and stops again, the myth still locked within the mind,
the closed and listless faces pulling out.

from *Colorado Review*

ANGELA SORBY

Museum Piece

◇　◇　◇

Now that your ship is ready, Susan, that hoop skirt sailing
down the aisle, a milk-white frigate of bound tits,

I must say congrats, you're "of age," he's nice and all that,
but I in my blue satin sausage skin want to stand

up and rage because there's been an end to courting
psychos by hitchhiking on Aurora, an end to splitting

one filched beer on the overpass in the dead of night.
Then, you smelled like a hundred hours of babysitting:

Pablum and cannabis. You'd steal my homework in a snap.
You were unwholesome, Susan. When I throw rice today,

I want to throw firecrackers and globs of canned frosting.
I want to throw COREY'S SLUG AND SNAIL DEATH in honor

of the toxic lawns in our parents' suburb. I want to jump up
during the ceremony, grab you and drag you back to our moral

vacuum, to watch your hair over and over like a blue
video: the way its long straight darkness swallows light.

But I shut up and grip my carnations. So this is how jinxed
card decks, blood feud bullets and lava-soaked cats end

up at the museum under glass. So we didn't O.D. or get slashed,
and now it's safe as school, it's folded up like a gossip note,

pale, pocket-sized, nothing that'd blow you away, this past.

from *The Nation* and *Kansas Quarterly*

The Nursery

◊   ◊   ◊

Rows of babies in plastic boxes,
faces red as worms freshly
brought forth from earth.
New elements in the vast disorder
swinging around them.

All the other lives
they will not lead
extinguished; labeled now,
they have been slotted
into place. Still wing-deep
in ether they push off,
constructing holograms
for others, beginnings
that brighten the rhythm
for the moment
for the rest of us
as when a crowd of cedar waxwings
making a gift of themselves,
net the tree with wild sounds,
flash their brief and beautiful greed.

They will march over meadows
hip-deep in yellow blossoms;
listen for winds from the south
to sweeten the path;
pick their ways through thickets
spangled like the breaths of panthers,
befuddled like us

by their weapons—
the faulty gestures they will
        brandish—
the stubborn convulsions of the heart.

They too will hear going by
what they have failed to find.
They will shelter always under
leaves splitting
the light and shadow
in patterns that cannot hold.

Lined up now like swimmers
in their lanes, eyes clenched.
Moorings cut
from the dream of zero
they are leaving, for a while.

                from *Witness*

Scatter

◇ ◇ ◇

Thank you for writing and we are happy
to respond to your inquiries.

Yes, it was Pericles who used the masts
of captured warships to build the Odeum;
Hugh Capet's son was Robert the Debonair,
and the Inca road system was comparable
to Rome's, but Romans had more words
for sex than Eskimos had for ice formations.
The air brake was invented in 1869,
the Rhetorical Wrench in 1844,
and "prurient" is the most quiet word
in the language, which is English,
and which, you'll be pleased to know,
happens to describe the afterlife
more relentlessly than most.
This should also be of interest to you
since, indeed, there is life after death,
even though it is extremely brief,
only a moment really; but keep in mind
that the closer you get to the sun
the slower time revolves, so
in that one sweeping moment
you may well get the chance
to tell your heart's desire
that she was made for the light

and hold each other as knowingly
as roses and grapevines
climbing the same sun-shot trellis.
Then, again, you may find yourself
giving a speech that enthralls
your audience but, because you have
no idea what the subject is, keeps you
clinging to the incomprehensible
like a fly to glass, until they
abruptly, inexplicably, shift
their attention with no loss
of intensity to the sight
of chimney smoke mingling with steam
from a nearby clothes drier vent,
or to a mutilated toad
the cat proudly presented,
or to drivers slowing down as you
did one spring afternoon
to watch two ancient sisters
emerge from their swayback house
to trim great, blooming, sail-high lilacs
in the same long-awaited wind that turns
the contrails of vanished planes
into night clouds thinner than the chalk
smears your swirling eraser wiped off
the blackboard behind you where beside
The Seven Lamps of Architecture,
The Seven Champions of Christendom,
Seven Pillars of Wisdom, Seven
Deadly Sins, Seven Liberal Arts,
Seven Sleepers of Ephesus, Seven
Sages of Rome, Seven Types
of Ambiguity, The Seven Wonders
of the Ancient and Modern World,
The Seven Sacraments, The Seven
Cities of Gold and The Seven Dwarfs,
you should have written The Seven

Sisters, The Seven Continents,
Seven Against Thebes, Seven Brides
for Seven Brothers, The Seven Samurai,
The Magnificent Seven and 7-Up.

from *Painted Bride Quarterly*

The Nose, the Grand Canyon, and the Sixties

◊　◊　◊

The curve of the path was to the left.
They followed it to the end though it had none;
Say, until they were tired.
Lace hung from their shoulders, some new,
Some crumbling, thick fur (was it wool?) was a common shawl
And the lace and the wool covered their chests and backs.
The lace may have been cotton. I'm here
It's far; it must have happened; it's far.
They made cotton. We met Jack Dempsey.
He said, You look like a nice couple, let me buy you a drink.
It was on the rim of the canyon, not in New York.
Days and their seconds passed on the beige trail.
The noise when a crowd runs was like the silence there:
When will it stop, oh when will it stop. Never.
In the force of a blow there is no pain,
It's more like meeting something irresistible
If you yourself are irresistible too.
Ever had a surprise party, a real surprise? Like that.
At night you told me a lie,
That a river ran through the center of the earth.
One had to be there, as I was, to believe it
Or want to believe it, its temperature, its grass.
Spanish horses in the thin woods knew before their riders
What was ahead, that it was singular and beyond power

And had a calm soul so they coughed and obeyed.
The men, jumpy, assumed the rest of the world from there on
Continued as canyons similar, overwhelming, and useless to China.
And reported that. A little blood and ice
And you're back to pretty and snorting after two weeks. A clean break.
Remember, a small party of five came up and out singing,
That sound as it first seemed, pieces of words
Pieces of letters, the tiny bit of dust almost not dust
Around them a half mile down when it seemed like barking
Or the survivors of a fight with space
Were moving toward us like metal bodies to fleshy magnets.

from *The Antioch Review*

DAVID WAGONER

Walt Whitman Bathing

◇ ◇ ◇

After his stroke, he would walk into the woods
On sunny days and take off all his clothes
Slowly, one plain shoe
And one plain sock at a time, his good right hand
As gentle as a mother's, and bathe himself
In a pond while murmuring
And singing quietly, splashing awhile
And dabbling at his ease, white hair and beard
Afloat and still streaming
Down his white chest when he came wading ashore
Naked and quivering. Then he would pace
In circles, sometimes dancing
A few light steps, his right leg leading the way
Unsteadily but considerately for the left
As if with an awkward partner.

He seemed as oblivious to passersby
As he was to his bare body, which was no longer
A nursery for metaphors
Or a banquet hall for figures of self-praise
But a bedroom or a modest bed in that bedroom
Or the covers on that bed
In need of airing-out in the sunlight.
He would sit down on the bank and stare at the water
For an hour as if expecting
Something to emerge, some new reflection
In place of the old. Meanwhile, he would examine
The postures of wildflowers,
The workings of small leaves, holding them close

To his pale eyes while mumbling inaudibly.
He would dress then, helping
His left side with his right as patiently
As he might have dressed the wounded or the dead,
And would lead himself toward home like a dear companion.

from *The Yale Review*

CHARLES H. WEBB

The Shape of History

◇   ◇   ◇

Turning and turning in the widening gyre . . .

Today's paper is crammed full of news: pages and pages on the Somalia
Famine, the Balkan Wars, Gays in the Military. On this date a year ago,
only ⅟₃₆₅ of "The Year's Top Stories" happened. *Time* magazine fits a
decade into one thin retrospective. Barely enough occurred a century
ago to fill one sub-chapter in a high school text. 500 years ago, one
or two things happened every 50 years. 5000 years ago, a city
was founded, a grain cultivated, a civilization toppled every
other century. Still farther back, the years march by in
groups like graduates at a big state university: 10,000 to
20,000 BC; 50,000–100,000 BC; 1–10 million BC.
Before that, things happened once an Era: Mam-
mals in the Cenozoic, Dinosaurs in the Meso-
zoic, Forests in the Paleozoic, Protozoans in
the Pre-Cambrian. Below that, at the
very base of time's twisting gyre, its
cornucopia,   its   ram's-horn   trum-
pet, its tornado tracking across
eternity, came what Chris-
tians call Creation, astro-
physicists call the Big
Bang. Then, for tril-
lions of years,
nothing at
all.

from *Michigan Quarterly Review*

ED WEBSTER

San Joaquin Valley Poems: 1969

◇   ◇   ◇

i. AFTER MAIL CALL

When my father wrote from the Tonkin Gulf about coyotes—
recollecting those he'd see on his way out
to the airfield, loping ahead on the quiet road
with their jokes of jackrabbit gristle—
my brother and I would wander, looking out
across soybean fields into tumbleweed and pogonip,
ignoring for a time the toads, to look
for bones, or anything telltale.
Finding nothing, we'd tally his *cat shots*
and pretend to fly, hurling ourselves into the air—
stock still to 130 in two seconds—
small warriors roaring over the flight deck,
ripping over rows of irrigation ditches
as we lost our father daily
to the Red River Delta.

ii. JUVENILIA

I remember writing a poem
when I was 7 or 8. It was printed up
at the grade school and my father was proud.
War is a terrible thing.
A pilot's fear is a burning wing. . . .

I catalogued everything I could remember
from movies. I rarely thought of it
later, even when a family friend
hurtled the length of the catapult
and exploded into the ocean. I never imagined
the great *Oriskany* fire, or later,
my father eyeing the tracer rounds drifting up
over Haiphong Harbor.
There were the distractions of summer.
It was life yet.

iii. AFTER READING JARRELL

Screwing down a jar lid,
I'm reminded of my father's fondness for peppers
and the old story about a spiced jar-full
gripping his guts at 30,000 feet.
"I had to think carefully
about what an A-4 was worth," he said.
I imagine him bringing the thing in
gingerly, and I can imagine as well his landing
at Da Nang with a rack full of hung bombs.
But he isn't one for trading stories,
and I'm mindful chiefly of a quiet
settling of accounts he mentioned once:
bringing death, daily bringing himself to death,
gone from his wife and gone from *the world*
where they marry and live in houses,
under the sky at sea and stars in unimagined numbers.

iv. IN LEMOORE

On summer afternoons, we'd set tumbleweeds on fire and fling
pomegranates at the empty water tower. Or crawling inside to
smash bottles, we'd press our hands against its rusting belly: I
remember the steel, slowly consumed by the air. But *do* I remember
that? This is all greatly what I imagine it to be. How do I remember
any mischief? What can I remember my father mentioning?

Only what he might have mentioned twenty years ago. I've remembered names of the valley: Iragaray, the Basque shepherd, singing next to his trailer, his sheep skittering a few paces under a sonic boom; Chavez, farther south, his name at Sunday mass coming round over rows of raisin paper, over whole furrowed fields laid out with drying raisins; Hubble, the Marine chaplain, home between tours; the Golden Dragons and all the squadron names. But what I remember of the boycotts, of the lettuce and the Teamsters, and what I remember of Tet—even the word *Tet*—are only open fields, the air shuddering, bright afternoons twisted with contrails.

v. A Token

I remember a dream moment: my father
unmoving in a chair, back straight
and his arms resting. Doors and windows
around him were open, and long curtains convulsed
with the air emptying
into the room.
        I take for a task
the description of that moment,
but it serves little to say *The air bloomed*
with its own scribbling particles.
There was no adequate epiphany, nothing
to cipher or read. But things did seem taken up
into the air; the exact moment was loosed
like a gaze fixed and everywhere at once: the world's things,
all I imagined then, were manifest, efflorescent
in that immense quiet, and everything not there
was felt. Everything not there was at least felt.

from *Western Humanities Review*

DAVID WOJAHN

Homage to Ryszard Kapuściński

◇ ◇ ◇

AESTHETICS: SAN MIGUEL FUTBOL STADIUM

Twenty thousand crowd into the gates—
Limón and tamales hawked from carts,

The mother, orbited by cameras, fidgets and waits
For her rebel son to die. The Junta must impart

Some lessons: let the people watch, let them dwell
On images.
        So Victoriano Gomez will be shot

By firing squad, on national TV. Martial
Music. Wind flings yellow helium balloons aloft.

Close up to the face: Victoriano, shackled and flanked
By twenty riflemen, shuffles from the locker room,

Is bound against a pole. . . .
        A captain yanks
The limp head up. The boyish faces of his doom

Shoulder their American M-16s. *Make them watch and make
Them think.* Make them watch and make them think.

Aesthetics II: Addis Ababa, 1976

"When he had seated Himself, I would slide
The pillow beneath His feet. Our Venerable

Majesty, it is well known, had a stature quite small.
Yet the Emperor Menelik's thrones were high,

Poorly suited for His tiny son. The Lion
Of Judah's Legs—
                    they could not *dangle* like a child's.

So I'd place my pillow with lightning speed,
Bowing as each Royal Audience began.

His pillow bearer thirty years!
                              Around the world
I went with Him, for protocol would demand

Each nation He'd visit to seat Him on a throne.
And for every throne I'd have a pillow made,

Its size and thickness measured exactly.
His Most Exalted Highness—
                        where could he go without me?"

Aesthetics III: Luanda Under Siege, 1975

Rebel forces have advanced to the outskirts.
Every night artillery fire,
                        even dog meat rationed.

The theatre owner's fled to Lisbon,
Deeding *Cine Mas* to his projectionist.

Just one film to show: *Emmanuelle.*
Over and over,
            eight shows a day, the house always full.

He freezes the film for the good parts. Catcalls,
Contemplation.
                        Heroic genitalia, eleven feet tall.

Start again, *stop*. Start again, stop. Klashnikov
And ack-ack fire. Emmanuelle and stranger on a plane.

Emmanuelle and several Kamasutra limber men.
Start again, *stop*. Orgasmic finale. Grenade going off

Down the block. Insult of multiple ironies:
The overturned Jeep, the six dead Cuban mercenaries.

THE FUNERAL OF KHOMEINI, 1989

Can we blame the mob for seeking holy relics,
A fragment from the Mullah's robe, a handkerchief,

Stained with His most precious blood? A copter must lift
The sainted coffin skyward:
                        the streets are too packed

For the hearses and the holy men to zigzag
Their path to the Saintly Tomb. The coffin's hooked,

A sea turtle, blundering toward air.
                                But the cables snap:
The turbaned body plummets like an oily rag

Doused with gas to set a house aflame.
Now begins the dark-robed conflagration,

Each chador a molecule, ravenous for oxygen,
Flaring white-hot. Now He is Theirs, and They are one,

Devouring Alpha and Omega, each face a frame
In a film with a cast of billions. The future belongs to Them.

TERMINUS: HOMAGE TO RYSZARD KAPUŚCIŃSKI

Fissured with trash, a lot in central Warsaw: the film
Is running, a documentary for the BBC,

Lenses trained on Ryszard Kapuściński,
Who has witnessed 27 revolutions.
                                    We watch him

Point to the spot where the station stood, the terminus
Where the cattle cars were loaded for the camps

(Treblinka was closest). Gesturing, he is flanked
By a gutted sofa and two fifty-gallon drums, the detritus

Of what the glib would label *history*,
The moment's dialectic with the past.

But nothing is so easy.
                        Now he squints,
And points beyond where the station stood. *You see*

That tire beside the stump? There stood the house
Where I was born. Only the past belongs to us.

from *Poetry*

228

JAY WRIGHT

The Cradle Logic of Autumn

◇ ◇ ◇

En mi país el otoño nace de una flor seca, de algunos pájaros . . .
o del vaho penetrante de ciertos ríos de la llanura.
MOLINARI, "Oda a una larga tristeza"

Each instant comes with a price, the blue-edged bill
on the draft of a bird almost incarnadine,
the shanked ochre of an inn that sits as still
as the beavertail cactus it guards (the fine
rose of that flower gone as bronze as sand),
the river's chalky white insistence as it
moves past the gray afternoon toward sunset.
Autumn feels the chill of a late summer lit
only by goldenrod and a misplaced strand
of blackberries; deplores all such sleight-of-hand;
turns sullen, selfish, envious, full of regret.

Someone more adept would mute its voice. The spill
of its truncated experience would shine
less bravely and, out of the dust and dunghill
of this existence (call it hope, in decline),
as here the blue light of autumn falls, command
what is left of exhilaration and fit
this season's unfolding to the alphabet
of turn and counterturn, all that implicit
arc of a heart searching for a place to stand.
Yet even that diminished voice can withstand
the currying of its spirit. Here lies—not yet.

If, and only if, the leafless rose he sees,
or thinks he sees, flowered a moment ago,
this endangered heart flows with the river that flees
the plain, and listens with eye raised to the slow
revelation of cloud, hoping to approve
himself, or to admonish the rose for slight
transgressions of the past, this the ecstatic
ethos, a logic that seems set to reprove
his facility with unsettling delight.
Autumn might be only desire, a Twelfth-night
gone awry, a gift almost too emphatic.

Logic in a faithful light somehow appeases
the rose, and stirs the hummingbird's vibrato.
By moving, I can stand where the light eases
me into the river's feathered arms, and, so,
with the heat of my devotion, again prove
devotion, if not this moment, pure, finite.
Autumn cradles me with idiomatic
certainty, leaves me nothing to disapprove.
I now acknowledge this red moon, to requite
the heart alone given power to recite
its faith, what a cradled life finds emblematic.

from *Callaloo*

Blue Guide

◇ ◇ ◇

> *"I'd like to retire there and do nothing."*
> ELIZABETH BISHOP

On this small island that undoes us daily, gently,
It's hard to take too seriously, too intently
A town whose name means *town*
(As well as *country, land,* and *nation*—
Exemplary synecdoche, one notes, even on vacation),
And which has just two buses
(One labors to and from the gritty port,
The other struggles to and from the smaller, higher town),
Each of which, when seen,
As usually, from a hill, inching up a slope or down,
Appears a cross between a donkey and a wind-up toy.
In cans, no less, the ferry brings in gasoline . . .
(It's hard, too, not to think of *you* in such outskirts . . .)
The gates to miniature courtyards
Before the two-room houses are just two feet high.
The bent and agéd widow in black crêpe,
Her groceries at her hip (as no doubt in her heart a sigh),
Must almost stoop to open them.

The one bus driver, who guides his glossy, truly verdigris
Mercedes from this main town to the country,
Is a kind of hero, according to Sabine
(Whose name rhymes with the French noun *cabinet,*
All that she, German, verb, wild, and self-exiled, seems not to be).

He has no room for error
On his steep way, so ever narrower
It is as though his wheels ran on a track.
They *should* be on a track.
There are few children of school age here,
And so on any given bus ride the fates of many
Are in his hands, both on the wheel.
From his one rearview mirror dangles
A silken, tangle-tasseled noose of amber worry beads,
A pale and bruised (or smudged) Saint Christopher,
An "eye," or *máti*, as they say in Greek—
Even more circumspectly apotropaic,
With its three ovals of white paint
Around the oval smalt glass bead recalling the Graeae.
Into an indentation in his dash
(Where a clock would go, if there were time)
Someone has pasted Jesus as a sugary shepherd.
In tourist season he'll pack thirty souls
Into this vehicle whose capacity, so its doors state,
Is fourteen. Now and then, the van must stop, must wait
For a herd of goats or a straggle of donkeys and *their* driver
To let it have the oxbow in the road.

When he is at the helm he does not smoke,
Though lounging in the shady square in Chóra
(*Chóra . . . chóra . . .* in the *Timaeus* womb and home
Of everything that moves and changes form),
Where he seems so out of his element, alert
And nervy as a sailor after his long voyage,
Ears plugged with last year's Walkman,
He works his beads through like a penitent and smokes,
Smokes like a fuse . . . But he never jokes,
And one cannot imagine him, unlike the town's
Other several Kostases (Kostádes?),
Sipping an endless watered ouzo,
Of an evening, whose sweet cloudiness,
The product of opposing clarities,
He can't afford the licorice vestiges of—
The lickerish, languid, lackadaisical effects of.

So when Iríni, lost in her twelve-year-old dreams of love,
Doesn't disembark, he knows—and calls her forth.
He has black, curly hair, thick as with suint, a thick mustache.
Vigilant, he wears dark, dark sunglasses with thin gold rims
Against the vigilant sun.

The other driver—like his van's springs—is bouncier.
He has a smile that shows off one gold eyetooth.
He has his amulets as well: a gilt cross,
A pair of fuzzy dice, elephantoid, a string of olive beads,
And then—isn't it?—a ceramic garlic bulb.
His bus is two-tone: jaded yellow over faded brown.
He drives toward sunrise, as Kóstas toward sunset.
And back, of course—they both drive back,
Each to his end of town.

One never sees the two together.
But they are brothers—maybe twins, but *unmistakably* they're
        brothers—
Even here where everyone's related.
Unless there are not really two of them.
So could there be one brother, as it were, in different modes?
If there are two, the one who flashes glinting smiles
And has a three-note horn he blows on his arrival
Has neatly lettered advertisements in his van:
"Hotel Odysseas," "Atalantides Souvenirs," "Caïque from Yannis"
(Calligraphy in the same hand).
There are no solicitations in the other bus,
There being no place visitors would want to stay, so many miles
From any shop, though there are still some residents
In the high village, its dwellings clinging to the road.
(For centuries the governments have made it the abode
Of favorite scapegoat dissidents.
It's one thing that this unknown place is known for.
One thing I think of *your* approving in it,
This isle that's still an exile,
Come to seem the perfect home
For certain types, who wouldn't—couldn't—change,
And yet who *needed* change, demanded *change* . . .)

233

Dimítrios makes change. Dispenses tickets—
After the ride, in careful trade for fare—
As though his ride alone were not worth 20 cents.

Our dourer driver does not deal out useless stubs.
He will provide directions,
Since there are several paths that lead off from his road.
There is the path to Déndro, or Tree, where on some days
On the horizon islands ride at anchor in a lavender haze
(Itself a product of opposing clarities),
And other days in the penumbra of the sky and sea
The only island that an eye can see
Is the idea of an island, forming for the very gaze,
Rather like *idea* in the Attic verb *to see*,
Precipitating itself, viewed as though through gauze,
As vague as *its* Greek source through *Tiffany*.

Another path leads to Angáli, and then, beyond some rocks,
There's a sliver of a beach where, on any given day,
The hiker might find Sabine.
A sort of tutelary spirit, ageless,
Although by now pure body, like a fish,
She eats the island's bread and bitter olives,
Drinks its raki, knows its coverts for the night,
And walks barefoot as though in boots
Through donkey dung and loose sharp rock.
Suddenly she stood,
In surf suds washing ankle bracelets,
Browned all over, blond hair sunbleached wheat and white,
Facing the sun, hands piling her hair up—
And when she turned, tufts of shining copper filaments.

There is the path to Zodóchos Pygi, the Church of the Fountain of
        Life,
A chastened venue, blued, sparely furnished—
No blind mouths here—
Although the name, when said aloud,
Calls up an animal, a stuffed (or stuffy) cartoon character.
There has to be as well a path to that white chapel,

234

Distant, guarded on one side
By what must be the island's only six Italian cypresses.
It looks like *the* local example, oddly estranged,
Of architecture ecclesiastical.
But then when one can't find it on the map at all,
It seems it was a crisp mirage.

Some paths fray out in scrub and friable hardscrabble.
Life is tough, says the thistle—and the furze says so too.
(Life is tough, the stone groans back, as the plants squeeze through.)

And there's a broad path to the Church of Pandelídhis,
Cobbled with stones the shades of almonds and pistachios.
As smooth as used soap bars,
As sucked-on lozenges, and sweetly modulated,
They make the spirit's dry mouth water for watercolors.
The church itself is painful white in sun,
And in the wind the courtyard's two bay laurels
Happily make their gull-like noises,
And dry leaves scramble crablike back and forth
Across the old stones outlined freshly with white paint.

The wind gusts up there, scented with sage, or thyme,
And blows away like gossip on the square.

Zigzagging up from Chóra there's the path to the Panaghía,
The church of the Madonna, perched above all else,
In daylight irresistible as a Carême meringue,
Within whose shadow for a moment one might think—
So this is where I've always meant to be:
Near these eroding ruins of a Venetian aerie,
At cliff's edge, just above where someone, not long ago,
Risking a neck to do it, built a little course of stones,
And set an orange crate in it.
And this is where I want to stay (so one might think),
Spying, or overseeing, really, *speculating*,
Essentially *episcopal*, and therefore *skeptical*,
Painting, drafting, drifting off in misty blue,
Doing the nothing special,

The special nothing one was born and bred to do.
Surrounded by outcroppings splashed with lichen,
Orange, pinkish, gray, and charcoal
(Or thriving, aging, dying, dead),
Among the goat turds like large coffee beans,
Letting the wind flip through *Geography III*
(Since I'd have nothing if not time),
I'd watch the azure sea
Turn up like plowed-down sillions in white water,
Muse on the mazy alleys down in town,
Follow a thought beyond that shotgun blast of bougainvillea,
Sudden and unanswerable as a ruptured aneurysm,
Beyond the very corner first
Turned—when? thirty years ago by now?—
That juncture where I slipped somehow
Into this iridescent bubble of the future
Waiting itself to burst . . .

And I would know how in the notebook
Were seeds of all the verse I'd ever want to make,
The poems it would take forever to have made,
Not one day more or less,
Poems modeled on the Wandering Islands,
A constellation of them, like the Kykládes, but in motion,
An archipelago loosely kaleidoscopic
Called sometimes "Neighborhood of a Point,"
Sometimes—less mathematically—"The Klitórides," or
        "Little Hills" . . .

How slow the evening is down there, beneath the Panaghía,
Where by now the chickens turn on their rotisseries,
Popping, popping—like the men out shooting *trigoniá*;
Where, later, deep in his taverna, Níkos clears up mysteries
(*Ah, naí, tó nekrotapheío*—the cemetery);
Where next door to my house a single workman paves
A courtyard with that seastone that's a kind of glaucous slate,
The Aegean's color on a cloudy day (with ingrained waves).
One family specializes in the cutting of it in the north
And in the southern shaping of it into those thin plates.
How quiet everything is here,

As quiet as the deepened light.
If you could scoop a little of it up—the light, the quiet—
The lucid color of a sapphire of first water
Like water in your hands . . .

But then, always before you're ready for it,
It is dark. It is dark . . .

Though if you stay there long enough you might meet Sabine.
If you do, maybe she'll go with you,
As the stucco glows brighter and colder,
Through the gates, and show you how to climb the church,
And where to lie down on the dome
(By now the whitewash is like sculpted snow,
Her burnished tones, by moonlight, a moontan),
And pick out patterns that the stars pick out.
What happens next is always pure improvisation.

Before departing, take the green bus out to its last stop,
Where Kóstas can point out an extravagant path
That finally reaches the island's tip,
Ambéli, or Vineyard,
Paradise at the world's end,
With tiny gardens lifted from the *Georgics*—
Gardens quite distinct (like the Islands of the Blesséd
In the Age of Gold, when *death* meant sleep as rich as honey,
When *food* meant honey, fruit, and vegetables),
Gardens of persimmon, quince, edged with shady olive trees
(The olive trees unpaintable, indeed, unprintable,
Moving in the barest breeze
As though a rain were falling silkily—
Although it's not: see, there are Virgil's bees),
Grapevines, melons, sweet corn, while bamboo sweeps the sky,
Sweet water runs on the surface, small frogs jump,
And (I swear) cows graze—and one crow always sits on one cow's
          rump
(Unless the crows take turns).
And from the beach (since here there's always time)
You must swim to the caverns,
As quickly cold as death, to cadge from Sabine,

237

Who takes you in to where,
As in some mad Cyclopic ear, black water gurgles,
Sloshes, slaps, and echoes, re-echoes . . .

But it's a matchless brilliant of a bay
You gasp back out to, the beach no bigger than a minute
(As someone in the family used to say),
Wherein the water's bezel of beryl green,
The blues our small Earth is from lunar vantage, marine
Mixed with milori, maybe, or blue turquoise—or is it
Berlin blue? or Brunswick blue?
Or since from my own point of view
The changing hue is so somehow suffused with *you*,
Bishop blue—is flat exquisite.

from *The Paris Review*

CONTRIBUTORS' NOTES AND COMMENTS

MARGARET ATWOOD was born in Ottawa, Ontario, in 1939. She was educated at Victoria College, the University of Toronto, Radcliffe College, and Harvard University. Her most recent collection of poems is *Morning in the Burned House* (Houghton Mifflin, 1995). Her novels include *The Handmaid's Tale* (1985), *Cat's Eye* (1989), and *The Robber Bride* (Doubleday, 1993). *The Handmaid's Tale* was adapted for the screen by Harold Pinter; the film was directed by Volker Schlöndorff and released in 1990. Atwood has edited *The New Oxford Book of Canadian Verse in English* (Oxford University Press, 1982), *The Best American Short Stories* (Houghton Mifflin, 1989), and *The Oxford Book of Canadian Short Stories in English* (Oxford University Press, 1986). She lives in Toronto, Canada.

Of "Bored," Atwood writes: "This is one of a series of poems on my father and his death—published in *Morning in the Burned House*. The details are from my assistant wood-sawing, house-building, etc., as a child in northern Quebec."

SALLY BALL was born in Summit, New Jersey, in 1968. She received an M.F.A. from Warren Wilson College in 1994 and has taught at Milton Academy and Beloit College. She has lived in Massachusetts and Illinois, and now lives in St. Louis with her husband, T. M. McNally.

Of "Nocturnal," Ball writes: "I wrote the first draft of this poem in Paul's Coffee Shop in Durham, New Hampshire, at a time when I wanted to defy my sense that I wouldn't have the privacy or presence of mind to write anything for another six months at least. It's one of a number of poems in which I've been figuring out how to use narrative (when really I am most seduced by the lyric moment), how to get a narrative to support—and then fall back quietly behind—lyric observation."

CATHERINE BOWMAN was born in El Paso in 1957. Her collection of poems *1-800-RIBS* (Gibbs Smith, 1993) won the Peregrine Smith Poetry Prize and the Kate Frost Tufts Discovery Award for Poetry. Her work was included in the 1989 and 1994 editions of *The Best American Poetry*. She lives and teaches in New York City.

Of "Mr. X," Bowman writes: "It was July and I was sitting on the beach in Port Aransas, Texas, watching the dolphins and the offshore oil rigs that line the horizon. George Jones came on the radio singing his country-western hit, 'All My Ex's Live in Texas.' I drew an *X* in the sand. A wave washed over it. I drew another *X*. A wave covered that one up, too. The waves were breaking that morning in sets of six. Six waves. Six *X*'s. Just the right number for a sestina. Eventually, I came up with this poem—a broken sestina to hold my broken heart. The poem's sixty *X*'s and *X*-sounds are the little stitches that mend it again and again. I had a lot of fun writing most of this poem, pretending to use the pretty Easter-egg pink embroidery thread left over from childhood that I'm partial to, part of the cross-stitch sampler that decorates my darling's and my nuptial kitchen."

STEPHANIE BROWN was born in Pasadena, California, in 1961, and grew up in Newport Beach. She has degrees from Boston University, the University of Iowa Writers' Workshop, and the University of California at Berkeley. Her work has appeared in *The Best American Poetry 1993*. "Schadenfreude" is from a manuscript entitled "Fitness." For several years she has worked as a public librarian in San Juan Capistrano, California. She lives in nearby San Clemente with her husband and their two small sons.

Of "Schadenfreude," Brown writes: "I wrote this poem and it sat in a file on the hard drive of my computer for about seven years before I rescued it and rewrote it (the computer creaked and the hard drive crashed soon after). My original idea was to write a poem as slapstick, with the funniness and cruelty of farce. I was also thinking of movies like *Texas Chainsaw Massacre* and Brian De Palma's version of *Scarface* and some grade-Z exploitation flicks I'd seen. While I don't particularly *like* these movies, they have fascinated and bothered me, making me both laugh and gasp in horror. When I revised the poem seven years later I first gave it the new title 'Schadenfreude,' which seemed to allow the poem to rewrite itself. It was originally written from an 'I' point of view and was changed to a 'you' attack (an illustration of psychological projection?). I was in the middle of an obsession with Alfred Hitchcock and reading and thinking a lot about the Jungian concept of the Shadow. None of the above passionately interests me anymore.

"*Schadenfreude* is a useful concept: the passive pleasure gained from someone else's misfortune. It's kinder and easier to accept in oneself than sadism, which perhaps few of us are capable of. I was thinking of our personal lives: the satisfaction one gets after watching hubris topple that one unbearable person who plagues our days—the phoney-baloney, the braggart, the sore loser, the mean-spirited, the humorless, the back-stabber, the sadist. It may take a while, but as surely as young George of *The Magnificent Ambersons* got his, they all get their comeuppance."

LEWIS BUZBEE was born in San Jose, California, in 1957. A graduate of the M.F.A. program at Warren Wilson College, he has made his living as a bookseller and publisher. Until recently he was a sales representative for Chronicle Books. Last year he gave up the "glamorous life of hotel rooms and highway rest stops" to stay home; now he teaches, writes, caters, "whatever." He has published one novel, *Fliegelman's Desire* (Ballantine Books, 1990). His interviews with Raymond Carver in *The Paris Review* and *The Bloomsbury Review* have been widely anthologized. "Sunday, Tarzan in His Hammock" is his first published poem.

Of "Sunday, Tarzan in His Hammock," Buzbee writes: "For me the spring of 1993 was a particularly lackluster time. I spent most of my weekends on the couch watching bad television. During this time, I became a regular watcher of a new live-action Tarzan series that was quite awful. I was jealous of Tarzan; he never seemed to have a bad day and was always saving the world. One Sunday, I roused myself from my torpor, went to my desk (all the way in the other room!), and squeezed out enough energy to write the title of the poem on a Post-it, after which I returned, exhausted, to my couch. That summer, when my writing had returned, I drafted the poem. The poem is my revenge against Tarzan and cheerful aerobics instructors everywhere."

CATHLEEN CALBERT was born in Jackson, Michigan, in 1955. Her poems have appeared in *Feminist Studies*, *The Paris Review*, *The New Republic*, *Shenandoah*, and *Western Humanities Review*. In 1991

241

she was awarded *The Nation*/Discovery Prize. She is an assistant professor of English at Rhode Island College in Providence, Rhode Island.

Of "The Woman Who Loved Things," Calbert writes: "I think the title came to me first, and I wrote a poem in response to it. Some of my feelings about our culture's consumerism and religious fanaticism went into the writing. This odd little fairy tale did not develop logically for me, or perhaps it developed its own logic. Maybe it just surprised me."

RAFAEL CAMPO was born in Dover, New Jersey, in 1964, and spent his childhood in northern New Jersey, with four years in Venezuela. He is the eldest son of a Cuban immigrant father and an Italian mother. He attended Amherst College and then Harvard Medical School; taking a year off from medicine, he studied poetry at Boston University as the George Starbuck Poetry Fellow. He finished his first manuscript, *The Other Man Was Me* (Arte Publico Press, 1994), before returning to his fourth year of medical school. Currently a resident in internal medicine at the University of California at San Francisco, he has written a second book of poems, *What the Body Told*, which Duke University Press will publish in 1996. A book of essays, *The Poetry of Healing: A Doctor's Education in Empathy, Identity, and Desire*, will appear from Norton in the fall of 1995.

Campo writes: "I wrote 'The Battle Hymn of the Republic' after hearing the moving story of Jose Zuniga, a much-decorated officer in the United States Army who was summarily discharged after revealing his homosexuality on National Coming Out Day, October 11, 1993. As a child of immigrants myself, raised as I imagine he must have been, with an ardent and abiding love of the freedoms afforded by this great country, I had once aspired to military service—but quickly reconsidered when I learned that my homosexuality was incompatible with the government's discriminatory policies. Instead, I chose a career nearly as repressive and regimented: medicine. Writing the poem was therapeutic for me, an antidote to the isolation I felt within my own profession as I struggled to be 'out' during my training—which meant anything from speaking up when an attendant made homophobic remarks about a patient dying of AIDS to slow-dancing with my partner of ten years in front of colleagues at departmental functions. It was also a gesture toward the loving community I knew must exist somewhere in the outside world. Barred from expressing my patriotism because of one facet of my identity, I felt I could finally fulfill that impulse by giving voice to, and defending, a nation that *would* have me. The poem is dedicated to Jose Zuniga and the thousands of gay and lesbian people who continue to serve their country, bravely but in silence."

WILLIAM CARPENTER was born in Boston in 1940, and grew up in Maine. He is the author of three books of poetry: *The Hours of Morning* (University of Virginia Press, 1980), *Rain* (Northeastern University Press, 1985), and *Speaking Fire at Stones*, a collaboration with the graphic artist Robert Shetterly. He has written a novel, *A Keeper of Sheep* (Milkweed, 1994). He has taught at the University of Chicago and the College of the Atlantic, where he served for several years as faculty dean. He has received a National Endowment for the Arts grant, the Associated Writing Programs Award, and the Samuel French Morse prize.

Of "Girl Writing a Letter," Carpenter writes: "I set out to produce a sad, straightforward elegy about the big art theft at the Gardner Museum in Boston. When I started writing, however, the girl stole the heart of the poem the same way her heart had been stolen by the thief. The crime has still not been solved."

NICHOLAS CHRISTOPHER was born in New York City in 1951. He is a graduate of Harvard College. He is the author of four books of poems: *5° & Other Poems* (1995), *In the Year of the Comet* (1992), *Desperate Characters: A Novella in Verse & Other Poems* (1988), and *A Short History of the Island of Butterflies* (1986), all from Viking Penguin. He has written two novels, *The Soloist* (Viking, 1986) and *Veronica*, forthcoming from the Dial Press in 1996. He has edited two anthologies, *Under 35* (Anchor, 1989) and *Walk on the Wild Side* (Scribner, 1994), and is currently at work on a book about film noir, entitled *Somewhere in the Night*, which will be published by the Free Press. He received a Guggenheim Fellowship for 1993–94. He lives in New York.

Christopher writes: "The facts in 'Terminus' are drawn from a true story. I believe the poem best speaks for itself."

JANE COOPER was born in Atlantic City in 1924 and grew up in rural north Florida and Princeton, New Jersey. She has published four books of poems. *The Weather of Six Mornings* (Macmillan, 1969), which was the 1968 Lamont Selection of the Academy of American Poets, was followed by *Maps and Windows* (Macmillan, 1974), *Scaffolding: Selected Poems* (Tilbury House, 1993), and, most recently, *Green Notebook, Winter Road* (Tilbury House, 1994). She has received fellowships from the Guggenheim and Ingram Merrill foundations. For many years she taught at Sarah Lawrence College, helping to develop its writing program. She lives in New York City.

Of "The Infusion Room," Cooper writes: "I have primary immune deficiency—which is mercifully different from acquired immune deficiency, or AIDS, in that you can grow old with it. But of course any immune deficiency implies a liability to infections. Specifically, I have some but not enough gamma globulin. Several years ago my life took a sharp turn for the better when I joined a group of patients at Mt. Sinai Hospital in New York City, all of whom receive intravenous doses of gamma globulin at regular intervals. For the first time I was introduced to other people who have what I have, or, rather, lack what I lack. To begin with, I was very allergic to the treatments, but nevertheless I would rush home after every session to write in my journal. I was so interested in the other patients and what I soon thought of as a shared culture. The Infusion Room could be likened to a small village square. In a limited area there is a bustle of activity and interchange: patients gossiping, nurses busy hitching up or monitoring IVs, doctors striding in and out, the television set on all day for distraction and white noise. Often a patient will be accompanied by a family member or a friend, who sits or stands along the wall as if to take up as little space as possible. Often the first effect of the infusion is to make us very sleepy. I was also new to daytime television and the riveting experience of hearing people's un-glib, real-life stories against a backdrop of talk-show testimony and 'All My Children.' Finally, I'm glad to have this opportunity to thank my doctor, Charlotte Cunningham-Rundles, M.D., Ph.D., of the Immuno-Therapy Group of the Division of Clinical Immunology at Mt. Sinai, senior clinical nurses Sarah Martin and Monica Reiter, medical technician Marilyn Guichardo, and my companions in the Infusion Room, named and unnamed."

JAMES CUMMINS was born in Columbus, Ohio, in 1948, and grew up in Indianapolis and Cleveland. He is curator of the Elliston Poetry Collection at the University of Cincinnati, where he teaches literature and writing. His first book, *The Whole Truth*, was published by North Point Press in 1986. He has received grants from the National Endowment for the Arts and the Ingram Merrill Foundation. He is no longer a baseball fan.

Of "Sestina," Cummins writes: "I wrote the first two stanzas of this poem, then put it away for two years. When I came across it again, I wanted to make the end words more challenging, and I did; 'neat' was harder to make work than 'Gary Snyder.' I wanted to write a story about two people who connect a little bit but mostly don't. I thought it would be amusing to have them on the fringes of lit'ry life. Of course, any resemblance to anyone living or dead is purely coincidental."

OLENA KALYTIAK DAVIS, a first-generation Ukrainian American, was born in Detroit in 1963 and spent her first twenty-one years there. Since then, she has lived in San Francisco, Prague, Lviv, Paris, and Chicago, and now lives in the isolated Yup'ik community of Bethel, Alaska. "Thirty Years Rising" is her first published poem.

Kalytiak Davis writes: " 'Thirty Years Rising' is obviously not autobiographical. In fact, it has nothing to do with me at all. Keep in mind what Plato said: 'Art can only reproduce at an angle.' One of the most heavily narrative and least lyrical of my poems, 'Thirty Years Rising' is also atypical in that it was felt before it was written and revised until no longer felt. Usually, the body is dead weight to the spirit. Usually, I don't use surrealism in service of personality. However, maybe it is typical of my work in that it addresses or at least nods toward a question I always seem to be asking: what if there is no distinction between reality and imagination?

"Speaking of exceptions to the rule, did I mention I don't believe in poets explicating their own work?"

LYNN EMANUEL was born in Mt. Kisco, New York, in 1949. She has lived, worked, and traveled extensively in Europe, the Middle East, and North Africa. Her most recent publication is a volume from the University of Illinois Press comprising her first book, *Hotel Fiesta*, and her second, *The Dig*. With David St. John she was poetry editor of a recent volume of *The Pushcart Prize Anthology*.

She is completing her third book, from which "Film Noir: Train Trip Out of Metropolis" is taken. She teaches English at the University of Pittsburgh.

Of "Film Noir: Train Trip Out of Metropolis," Emanuel writes: "This poem, from a sequence, is one moment in an extended, testy, affectionate argument I am having with the movies. I am using film noir to represent all of film because, like a poem, it is 'written' in black and white. The premise behind the sequence is that poetry and film are in the same position relative to one another today that painting and photography were in at the turn of the century. I am imagining that poetry has to reinvent its purpose in the face of a powerful technology that has abrogated many of its traditional functions. The sequence that surrounds 'Train Trip' begins by asserting, dourly, that the movies are—literally and figuratively—more moving than poetry. So, for me, the subject of this poem is not only the movies but also (and, perhaps, more importantly) motion and emotion."

ELAINE EQUI was born in Oak Park, Illinois, in 1953. Her most recent collection of poems, *Decoy*, was published by Coffee House Press in 1994. She lives in New York City and teaches at the New School, the Writer's Voice, and City College.

Of "Sometimes I Get Distracted," Equi writes: "To me, this poem really conveys the sometimes enormous difference between knowing something intellectually and knowing it experientially, i.e., being able to put it to use in your life. The central image of playing catch with a monk came out of a dream I had. As I had been rereading Philip Whalen at the time, I had no reservations about giving the whole poem a Zen-like flavor and dedicating it to him. He has always been a source of tremendous inspiration to me, particularly because of the way he is able to follow an idea through all its detours and cul-de-sacs without ever losing sight of the reader."

IRVING FELDMAN was born in Brooklyn, New York, in 1928. He is the author of *New and Selected Poems* (Viking Penguin, 1979), *All of Us Here* (Viking Penguin, 1986), and *The Life and Letters* (University of Chicago Press, 1994). In 1986 he received a grant from the National Endowment for the Arts, and in 1992 he was made a MacArthur Fellow. He traveled to Japan in 1994. He is Distinguished Professor of English at the State University of New York at Buffalo.

Of "Terminal Laughs," Feldman writes: "I hope that giving Gregory the last laugh absolves him of having taken the first sneer."

DONALD FINKEL was born in New York City in 1929. He is the author of fourteen volumes of poetry. *The Garbage Wars* (Atheneum, 1970) was nominated for the National Book Award. Both *A Mote in Heaven's Eye* (Atheneum, 1975) and *What Manner of Beast* (Atheneum, 1981) were nominated for the National Book Critics Circle Award. He has also published a book of translations, *A Splintered Mirror: Chinese Poetry from the Democracy Movement* (Northpoint Press, 1981). In 1980 he received the Morton Dauwen Zabel Award from the American Academy of Arts and Letters. Until 1991, he was poet-in-residence at Washington University in St. Louis. *Beyond Despair* (Garlic Press, 1994), a chapbook, received the 1994 Yearbook Award for poetry from the *Dictionary of Literary Biography*.

Of "In the Clearing," Finkel writes: "This poem grew out of a recent summer I spent in southern Vermont. The clearing, which has been created out of the scrubby woods that surrounded it, became for me a metaphor for the mysterious, unstable border between the natural world and what men have made of it. The poem is an exploration of that border between unconstrained nature and civilization with its attendant discontents."

AARON FOGEL was born in New York City in 1947. His books include *Chain Hearings* (Inwood/Horizon Press, 1976) and *Coercion to Speak* (Harvard University Press, 1985), a study of dialogue form in Conrad and scenes of forced dialogue in general. He received a Guggenheim Fellowship in 1987. He teaches at Boston University. His work appeared in the 1989 and 1990 editions of *The Best American Poetry*. Works-in-progress include a one-hundred-section novel with one hundred narrators called *The Centipede*, and a study of demographics and literature.

Of "The Printer's Error," Fogel writes: "As a professor I sometimes find misprints luminous, or at least a relief, in books I repeatedly teach. A vocational illness maybe: to believe that they're sacred hints or maybe intentional swipes by printers out of class anger. But Frank Steinman, with whom I first became friends late in

1961, had a version of this belief far more radical, developed, and thoughtful. When his wife, Bettie, wrote me, a few years after his death in 1988, to complain that his will and other writings were still being denied publication by all 'the powers that be,' and asked me to turn this one piece of prose into verse, so as to make it more publishable, I was more than ready to comply. I had and have some fear, though, that Frank's ideas are so much more radical than mine that my version will have unintentionally blunted some of the sheer brilliance and force of them. But I did my best. In any case, Mitch Sisskind, editor of *The Stud Duck*, courageously broke ranks with all the other editors, cowed by you know who, who were then daily pressuring him to keep Steinman's voice silent. I'm happy that readers on a mass scale can now have some hint, however diminished or tamed, of what Steinman's writing was really like. You all know what happened after the first appearance of Frank's testimony in *The Duck*: the reorganization of the printing industry in favor of the workers who produce the texts; the riots in the streets; the cataclysmic shift of power in universities toward admirers of Gertrude Stein; the replacement of the entire 'canon' by forced readings from *The Duck*; Steinman's apotheosis and the creation of a new religion (of which he himself would have disapproved) in his name; and on and on: all the good results that have followed from our allowing ourselves to listen for a moment to what an apparently simple working-class 'crank' printer had to say about the redistribution of meaning in the world."

RICHARD FROST was born in Palo Alto, California, in 1929. He is the author of *The Circus Villains* (1965) and *Getting Drunk with the Birds* (1971), both with Ohio University Press; the chapbook *Jazz for Kirby* (State Street Press, 1990); and *The Family Way* (The Devil's Millhopper Press, 1994). His new collection, *Neighbor Blood*, is ready for editorial perusal. He is a working jazz drummer and teaches English at the State University College in Oneonta, New York. He is married to the poet Carol Frost; they live in an old farmhouse in the Otsdawa Valley near Otego, New York, with their 1952 Buick and their cat and dog and assorted undomesticated animals.

Of "For a Brother," Frost writes: "That record, from my high school days, was by Louis Jordan and his Tympany Five. Somewhere I still have the old blue-label Decca 78. As for my one brother, my bedeviled hero, he smoked and drank his way to oblivion. I'll never escape him, never want to."

ALLEN GINSBERG was born in Newark, New Jersey, in 1926. In *Howl* (1956) he uttered the battle cry of the Beat movement; the poem was the subject of a 1957 obscenity trial in San Francisco. In the 1960s Ginsberg chanted mantras, sang poems, advocated peace and pot, and fused the influences of William Blake, William Carlos Williams, Eastern mysticism, and Hebrew prophecy in his work. Hearing Ginsberg read *Howl* hastened Robert Lowell's evolution into a confessional poet. Crowned May King in Prague in 1965, Ginsberg was expelled by Czech police and simultaneously placed on the FBI's list of subversives. His books from that period include *Kaddish* (1961), *Reality Sandwiches* (1963), and *Planet News* (1968). Recent collections are *Collected Poems 1947–1980* (Harper & Row, 1984), *White Shroud* (1985), and last year's *Cosmopolitan Greetings: Poems 1986–1992* (HarperCollins). Ginsberg is a member of the American Institute of Arts and Letters and co-founder of the Jack Kerouac School of Disembodied Poetics at the Naropa Institute in Colorado, the first accredited Buddhist college in the Western world. He has written the libretto for an opera, *Hydrogen Jukebox*, with Philip Glass's score. A volume of his *Journals 1954–1958*, edited by Gordon Ball, is forthcoming from HarperCollins. He is now Distinguished Professor at Brooklyn College.

Regarding "Salutations to Fernando Pessoa," Ginsberg directs the reader to Pessoa's "Salutation to Walt Whitman." Pessoa wrote poetry under several identities, or heteronyms: each was not simply a pen name but a distinctive personality he outfitted with a full life history. "Salutation to Walt Whitman" was written by the poet and sometime naval engineer Pessoa calls Alvaro de Campos. The poem begins in a suitably swaggering way: "From here in Portugal, with all past ages in my brain,/I salute you, Walt, I salute you, my brother in the Universe,/I, with my monocle and tightly buttoned frock coat,/I am not unworthy of you, Walt, as you well know . . ." A little later, brother and other become one: "Look at me: you know that I, Alvaro de Campos, ship's engineer,/Sensationist poet,/Am not your disciple, am not your friend, am not your singer,/You know that I am You, and you are happy about it!" See *The Poems of Fernando Pessoa*, translated by Edwin Honig and Susan M. Brown (Ecco, 1987), pp. 72–78.

PETER GIZZI was born in Alma, Michigan, in 1959 and grew up in the Berkshires. He holds degrees from New York University and Brown University. He is currently a Ph.D. candidate in the poetics program at the University of Buffalo and is editing *The Complete Lectures and Letters of Jack Spicer* for Black Sparrow Press. His first full collection, *Periplum: Or, I the Blaze*, was published in 1992 by Avec Books. He has three chapbooks: *Hours of the Book* (Zasterle, 1994), *Music for Films* (Paradigm, 1992), and *Creeley Madrigal* (The Materials, 1991). In 1986 he co-founded the literary magazine *O.blek*. In 1993–94 he was a visiting professor in English at Brown University, where he is currently a visiting scholar. He was recently selected by John Ashbery for the Peter I. B. Lavan Younger Poets Award from the Academy of American Poets.

Gizzi writes: " 'Another Day on the Pilgrimage' is primarily about grief and the difficult joy that comes from making something out of that space. In the process it creates a critique out of 'the everyday.' Even in the ordinary, figural law is duplicated and even the most anonymous activity is invested with a larger order no one escapes. The poem is an exercise in perspective; simply put, when we forget what we've lost we lose everything. The pilgrimage is a traversing through books, landscapes (real or imagined), and memories. The poem is meant to create the effect of how deserted this place is, and how the great potential that exists within emptiness can sometimes be revealed through language. 'Another Day on the Pilgrimage' is part of a work-in-progress entitled *A Textbook of Chivalry*. The act of chivalry in this instance is to create a speech that would never embarrass the dead."

JODY GLADDING was born in York, Pennsylvania, in 1955. Her first book, *Stone Crop*, was published in the Yale Younger Poets Series in 1993. A graduate of the Cornell University M.F.A. Program and a former Stegner Fellow at Stanford University, she lives near Montpelier, Vermont.

Gladding writes: "In 'Asparagus,' 'the country my mother still calls hers' is northern Germany, where she lived until 1947. 'Show me your face before you were born,' demands the Zen master. My question is less enlightened: 'Show me your face before *I* was born.' And always her answer remains both a commonplace and an enigma."

ELTON GLASER was born in New Orleans in 1945. He is a professor of English and director of the University of Akron Press, which began publication of the Akron Series in Poetry in 1994. Three full-length collections of his poems have been published: *Relics* (Wesleyan, 1984), *Tropical Depressions* (Iowa, 1988), and *Color Photographs of the Ruins* (Pittsburgh, 1992). Among his awards are two fellowships each from the National Endowment for the Arts and the Ohio Arts Council, the Iowa Poetry Prize, and the Randall Jarrell Poetry Prize.

Glaser writes: " 'Undead White European Male' is dedicated to Charles Simic because the poem was triggered as I read his book *Hotel Insomnia*. No specific poem served as a model, but something about Simic's dark comedy and Balkan atmosphere set me to writing this vampire piece. Puns ('More Parisian than parasite'), anagrams ('Saint of the satin afterlife'), and sheer linguistic tomfoolery ('Putting the frostbite on another frightened neck') keep the poem going in a playful mood that undermines the traditional treatment of this subject matter.

"Laszlo is no sinister creature of the night, but a bumbling, pitiful figure who, if he had a choice, would prefer to be in a different line of work. He seems particularly unsuited for his vocation in the age of AIDS and in a culture 'afraid of its own past.' The title came to me about two-thirds of the way through my composition, when I wanted the poem to settle into a more serious closure, so that these comic improvisations on a theme would not end arbitrarily but with a sharper sense of the inevitable. I wanted to put a little bite into these smiling lines.

"For me, Laszlo is a sympathetic character. This may be because the poem was such a pleasure to write. Or perhaps it is because, after nearly twenty-five years in Akron, I have come to feel a great affinity with the undead."

ALBERT GOLDBARTH was born in Chicago in 1948. His recent books include *Across the Layers: Poems Old and New* (University of Georgia Press), *The Gods* and *Marriage, and Other Science Fiction* (both from Ohio State University Press), and a volume of essays, *Great Topics of the World* (David R. Godine). He received the National Book Critics Circle Award for the collection *Heaven and Earth* (University of Georgia Press) and the *Beloit Poetry Journal* Chad Walsh Memorial

Award for his poem "The Two Domains." He is Distinguished Professor of the Humanities at Wichita State University.

Of "A Still Life, Symbolic of Lines," Goldbarth writes: "Every year I sound, even to my own self-empathetic ears, more curmudgeonly: refusing to trade in my beloved IBM Selectric for a computer; refusing to e-mail friends, in favor of actual (remember them?) letters; and now (as was true of my inclusion in the 1993 edition of this series) refusing to comment on the poem, which I believe ought properly to be self-sufficient and approached without gratuitous clutter. I suppose it's just the kind of comment that the author of just such a poem *would* write. Odd old bird."

BECKIAN FRITZ GOLDBERG was born in Hartford, Wisconsin, in 1954 and grew up in Arizona. She received her M.F.A. from Vermont College in 1985 and is the author of two books of poetry, *Body Betrayer* (1991) and *In the Badlands of Desire* (1993), both from Cleveland State University. She teaches at Arizona State University.

Of "Being Pharaoh," Goldberg writes: "On hot, tomb-still, late summer nights here the birds are insomniacs as I am. Maybe that's why the first harbinger of this poem was the image of a bird who'd been around so long a beard had grown from its beak. I wrote three seeming non sequiturs, in couplets; I had no idea where I was going. My notebook was full of bitching-as-usual about not being able to write. Over the next few nights, I felt I was simply moving from one thing to another the way my mind does anyway and I kept hoping I'd reach some point where I could feel reassured about what I was doing; I kept trying to 'wrap it up.' Each night I'd remain in the dark. I was finally ready to resign when the closing lines came to me simultaneously with the thought that I really shouldn't write such an ending."

LAURENCE GOLDSTEIN was born in Los Angeles in 1943. His three books of poetry include *The Three Gardens* (1987) and *Cold Reading* (1995), both from Copper Beech Press. His most recent book of literary criticism is *The American Poet at the Movies: A Critical History* (Michigan, 1994). He teaches English at the University of Michigan and edits *Michigan Quarterly Review*.

Of "Permissive Entry: A Sermon on Fame," Goldstein writes: "*Permissive entry* is a legal term referring to the consensual and unobstructed passage of persons into private property. (Its antonym is *forcible entry*.) The term lingered in my mind for several years before I thought to broaden its application, and the poem took shape as I jotted down illustrative cases (most of them omitted in the final version) of how often we enter unknowingly and permanently into other lives, haunting even strangers (as they do us) by unacknowledged interventions.

"In the semblance of an orderly argument, the poem proposes an unconventional way of thinking about fame—fame, that hobgoblin of the poet and succubus of every citizen in a media culture. The anxiety of being lost to history rather than buoyed up in the fluency of Time accounts for several allusions, like the incognito Bulkington from *Moby-Dick*. Like all sermons the poem seeks to construct and console."

BARBARA GUEST was born in Wilmington, North Carolina, in 1920. A longtime resident of New York City, she recently moved to Berkeley, California. "I can easily write, 'Poet returns to the scenes of her youth,' as I grew up in Los Angeles and graduated from the University of California at Berkeley. (At which point nostalgia for New York will overwhelm me.)" Her books of poetry include *Fair Realism* (Sun & Moon, 1989), *The Countess from Minneapolis* (Burning Deck, 1991), and *Selected Poems* (Sun & Moon, 1995). She has written a biography: *Herself Defined: The Poet H.D. and Her World* (1984).

Of "If So," Guest writes that it is "a poem of ambivalence, of my continued questioning of reality in what is largely a suppositional world where the real and the imagined collide."

MARILYN HACKER was born in the Bronx in 1942. In 1975 she won the National Book Award in poetry for *Presentation Piece*. Her seven other books include *Winter Numbers* and *Selected Poems 1965–1990*, both from Norton in 1994. In 1991 she received a Lambda Literary Award for *Going Back to the River* (Random House). She was the editor of *The Kenyon Review* from 1990 to 1994.

Of "Days of 1992," Hacker writes: "The Alcaic stanza with its Horatian as well as Attic overtones almost imposed itself on me for this meditation on the intersections of history and domesticity. For ten years now, I've lived at least part of every year in Paris, in the Marais, a neighborhood that's a palimpsest of European history, including, of course, the history of the Jews. Hundreds of Jewish immigrant victims of the mass arrests of July 1942 were my neighbors, or would be my neighbors had they not been deported and murdered. But 'Days of 1992' also became an elegy for a woman who *was* my neighbor, very much alive at 101 when I began the poem, who had died when I came back to it a year later: in the text, she lives still, with all her contradictions."

JUDITH HALL was born in Washington, D.C., in 1956. Her first book, *To Put the Mouth To* (William Morrow, 1992), was selected by Richard Howard for the National Poetry Series. For two years, she administered grants in literary publishing at the National Endowment for the Arts. She has taught at U.C.L.A. and St. Mary's College of Maryland.

Of "St. Peregrinus' Cancer," Hall writes: "The poem may be most indebted to the arcane *Watercolours of Cancer Patients' Dreams* (Phoebe Lord, M.D., London, 1964). Note, for example, from the women interviewed: 'In the beginning, mothers and daughters squeeze in patent leather spikes. They help each other rifle tumble tables, laughing in matching dresses, as they debate the lilac, chartreuse. Conversations turn, they die, and what was imagined isolates. Then will come this other sound, most useful and intimate when touching on their wounds. The wounds are love. They lunch' (29).

"From the men: 'What bothered him was his vasectomy the day before' (40); 'saints appear in cancer patients' dreams' (*xii*)."

ANTHONY HECHT was born in New York City in 1923. His B.A. from Bard College was granted in absentia (1944) while he was overseas with the army; he later earned his M.A. from Columbia University. After forty years of teaching at Bard College, Kenyon College, Smith College, the University of Rochester, Iowa State University, and Georgetown University, he retired in 1993. Most of his poetry has been assembled in *The Collected Earlier Poetry of Anthony Hecht* and *The Transparent Man*, both published by Knopf. His other works include *Obligatti: Essays in Criticism* (Atheneum); a critical study of W. H. Auden's poetry, *The Hidden Law* (Harvard University Press); *On the Laws of the Poetic Art: The Andrew Mellon Lectures, 1992* (Princeton, 1995); and *The Presumptions of Death* (Gehenna Press, 1995). He has received the Pulitzer Prize, the Bollingen Prize, and the Eugenio Montale Award. He and his wife live in Washington, D.C.

Of "Prospects," Hecht writes: "The villanelle form is truly challenging, and I avoided it for a long time, while admiring the successes of such practitioners as Elizabeth Bishop, William Empson, Dylan Thomas, James Merrill, Mark Strand, and W. H. Auden. Mine is a little pilgrimage or quest poem, as perhaps the industrial by-product of a set of poems written (in the paradisal setting of the Rockefellers' Villa Serbelloni at Bellagio) to accompany woodcuts by Leonard Baskin, and called *The Presumptions of Death*. The poem's title is meant to convey our very ambivalent feelings about the future, since 'prospects' can be hopeful, referring to financial profits, to favorable expectations in mining operations, but also can be fearful or troubled, and can neutrally refer to panoramic overviews and remote landscapes. The 'theme' to be heard in the 'pale paradigm of birdsong' at the end of the poem is meant to be the very faint echo, almost undetectable, of something hinted at in the opening lines: 'He maketh me to lie down in green pastures: he leadeth me beside the still waters.' If mountain streams are not, strictly speaking, 'still,' the lines in the psalm refer to 'the waters of quietude.' Implied, perhaps, but unstated: 'He restoreth my soul.' "

EDWARD HIRSCH was born in Chicago in 1950. He is the author of four books of poems, all from Knopf: *For the Sleepwalkers* (1981); *Wild Gratitude* (1986), which won the National Book Critics Circle Award; *The Night Parade* (1989); and *Earthly Measures* (Knopf, 1994). He teaches at the University of Houston.

Of "Unearthly Voices," Hirsch writes: "Hugo von Hofmannsthal (1874–1929) wrote all his lyric poetry before he was twenty-six years old. He then abandoned poetry and concentrated on essays, prose fiction, and plays. Hofmannsthal traveled to Greece in 1908 with his friends Count Kessler and the French sculptor Maillol. My poem derives most immediately from the first section of his essay 'Moments in Greece.' It may be useful to think of the poem taking place at the historic moment when the gods turn into a single God."

JANET HOLMES was born in Libertyville, Illinois, in 1956. She was educated at Duke University and Warren Wilson College. She has received a Bush Foundation Artist's Fellowship and a Minnesota State Arts Board grant, and currently teaches at the Loft in Minneapolis. Her collection *The Physicist at the Mall* won the Anhinga

Poetry Prize (Anhinga Press, 1994), and a chapbook, *Paperback Romance*, was published by State Street Press in 1984. She recently completed a manuscript called "The Green Tuxedo." A. R. Ammons chose her work for *The Best American Poetry 1994*. She lives in St. Paul, Minnesota, with her husband, the poet Alvin Greenberg.

Of "Against the Literal," Holmes writes: "Though it's been four years since I lived in New Mexico, its landscape continues to haunt my dreams and my poems. I was forewarned about this by my friend Harriet Cole, who first taught me the 'camp robber' nickname for the pinyon jay—a bold and friendly bird who will make himself comfortable in your camp to the extent of helping himself to some of your lunch even while you are in the midst of eating. Gray jay, too, is a name I've seen given to this bird, though a woman who's written a Ph.D. dissertation on pinyon jays assures me there are subtle distinctions between the two.

"I was fortunate in having editors like Stan Lindberg and Stephen Corey, who suggested minor but important revisions in this poem before it was published."

ANDREW HUDGINS was born in Killeen, Texas, on the Fort Hood army post, in 1951, and was raised on and near air force bases in the United States and abroad, but primarily in the South. He attended high school, college, and graduate school in Alabama before doing more graduate work at Syracuse University and the University of Iowa. His four books, all published by Houghton Mifflin, are *Saints and Strangers* (1985), *After the Lost War* (1988), *The Never-Ending* (1991), and *The Glass Hammer: A Southern Childhood* (1994). He teaches at the University of Cincinnati.

Of "Seventeen," Hudgins writes: "To the extent I grew up at all, I grew up in Alabama, and the Deep South is, as the anthropologists say, a courtesy culture. One of the hardest things I had to learn through my teens and twenties was to deal with adults as equals. At twenty-five I was still addressing waitresses with the obsequious 'Yes ma'am' and 'No ma'am' of a child—a habit I was able to break only when I noticed my deference was making them uncomfortable or even angry. The poem 'Seventeen' is about an earlier and more dramatic rite of passage.

"The poem was originally part of a short story, the product of a misbegotten and reckless youth. When I was writing my most recent book, *The Glass Hammer: A Southern Childhood*, I went back to that fifteen-year-old story, found this passage, and recast it as a poem."

T. R. HUMMER was born in Macon, Mississippi, in 1950. He edited *The Kenyon Review* (1988–89) and *New England Review* (1989–93). He is the author of four books of poetry, most recently *The 18,000-Ton Olympic Dream* (William Morrow, 1991). He received a Guggenheim Fellowship in 1993. He is the director of the creative writing program at the University of Oregon in Eugene, where he lives.

Hummer writes: " 'Apocatastasis Foretold in the Shape of a Canvas of Smoke' took shape out of a years-long meditation on and against the gnarly, artificial, and difficult-to-get-away-with-using-in-a-poem word *apocatastasis*. The first poem I ever published in a national literary magazine—a labored and turgid sonnet in homage to Gerard Manley Hopkins—has *apocatastasis* in its concluding line. In 1971, when that poem was written, I was dissatisfied with the intrusiveness of all those Grecian syllables into a poem which was laboring to be, à la GMH, Anglo-Saxon, accentual, and sprung. What I could not know then was that my rhythmic problem with the bizarre music of the word was a mask for larger issues, more irreducible problems, which the present poem begins to dramatize, if not to solve.

"*Apocatastasis* is defined by one unabridged dictionary as (1) the state of being restored or reestablished; restitution; (2) the doctrine that Satan and all sinners will ultimately be restored to God. From Greek: a setting up again. In terms of Christian theology, apocatastasis is the restoration of everything broken by time and history in the fallen cosmos after the second coming of Christ. It is a beautiful, mysterious word—who can say exactly what it meant to the Greeks?—to which has been grafted a sentimental and reductive concept that collapses the whole of human existence, strictly speaking, to comedy. The poem 'Apocatastasis Foretold in the Shape of a Canvas of Smoke' arises out of my indignation against such an easy erasure of pain, and my obsession therefore with deploying the language of mysticism against itself.

"But the immediate trigger to the writing of this poem was a walk with a friend in the course of which we passed a yard where an old woman in a gray dress was dumping something undefinable out of a galvanized steel bucket while a dog, exactly the same color as the bucket, skulked at her ankles. There was something so thoroughly timeless in this tableau that it defeated, for a microsecond, all my time-bound notions about the value of human existence, or the lack thereof. Tragic? Comic? Mystic? Who cares? In a universe where things are forever set up and knocked down and set up again, *apocatastasis* simply means that there is always work to be done."

BRIGIT PEGEEN KELLY was born in Palo Alto, California, in 1951. *To the Place of Trumpets*, her first book, was published by Yale University Press in 1988; her second book, *Song*, was published by BOA Editions in 1995. She teaches creative writing at the University of Illinois at Champaign-Urbana.

KARL KIRCHWEY was born in Boston in 1956 and grew up in the United States, Canada, England, and Switzerland. A Yale graduate, he received an M.A. in English literature from Columbia. His books of poems include *A Wandering Island* (Princeton, 1990), which won the Norma Farber First Book Award from the Poetry Society of America, and *Those I Guard* (Harcourt, Brace, 1993). Since 1987 he has been the director of the Unterberg Poetry Center of the 92nd Street YM–YWHA in New York City. He has held a Guggenheim Fellowship. He spent 1994 in Rome on a fellowship from the American Academy of Arts and Letters.

Of "Sonogram," Kirchwey writes: "The immediate occasion of this poem is evident from the title. In April 1992, my wife and I received a glimpse *in utero* of our first child, a boy named Tobias who was born in September of that year. My emotions at witnessing this procedure were twofold. On the one hand, the medical sophistication of it, and the audacity of being able to view such hidden things, seemed so astounding that the only adequate response was through the imagination—the metaphors by which the parts of the body are described—in the form of a prayer. My other emotion, which also justified prayer, was anxiety, since the chief purpose of a sonogram is to detect birth defects in the fetus.

"Traveling in Sicily years ago, I had walked through the deep ancient quarries at Syracuse, now full of citrus trees but once an open-air prison in which thousands of Athenian soldiers died of exposure and disease during the Peloponnesian War in September 413 B.C. The cultural critic and historian George Steiner has written,

'The quarries of Syracuse have long signaled that in the lotteries of the unpredictable it is disaster that has all the luck.' And it was the image of these quarries, and their shadowed promise, which suggested itself last in the little catalogue of images I offered my then-unborn son as I contemplated the life that lay ahead of him.''

CAROLYN KIZER was born in Spokane, Washington, in 1925. A graduate of Sarah Lawrence College, she studied poetry with Theodore Roethke at the University of Washington. She worked for the State Department as a literature specialist in Pakistan and was, from 1966 to 1970, the first director of the Literature Program of the National Endowment for the Arts. She has taught at Columbia, Iowa, Cincinnati, Stanford, and Bucknell. Her books include *The Ungrateful Garden* (1961), *Knock Upon Silence* (1965), *Midnight Was My Cry* (1971), *Yin: New Poems* (BOA Editions, 1984), and *The Nearness of You* (Copper Canyon, 1987). *Yin* won the Pulitzer Prize. She is the editor of *The Essential Clare* (The Ecco Press, 1992) and *100 Great Women Poets* (Ecco, forthcoming 1995). She divides her time between Sonoma, California, and Paris.

Of "On a Line from Valéry," Kizer writes: "This villanelle is, of course, a response to the Gulf War, and was circulated in manuscript to other poets who also responded. On the train returning from a reading in Portland the day after the war began, when yellow ribbons were everywhere, I saw through the train window a large black flag hanging from a porch in Eugene, Oregon. I wanted to jump off the train and embrace the person who had hung it there. The poem of Valéry from which the line was taken was one that had been discussed in a translation class I was teaching at Davis just then. This is my third villanelle in thirty years; I've always liked the form for its use of reiterated lines, so suited to obsessive subjects and strong passions.''

WAYNE KOESTENBAUM was born in San Jose, California, in 1958. He was educated at Harvard, Johns Hopkins, and Princeton. He has published two books of poetry, *Rhapsodies of a Repeat Offender* (1994) and *Ode to Anna Moffo and Other Poems* (1990), both from Persea. He is also the author of *The Queen's Throat: Opera, Homosexuality, and the Mystery of Desire* (Poseidon, 1993), which was nominated for a National Book Critics Circle Award, and *Jackie Under My Skin: Interpreting an Icon* (Farrar, Straus and Giroux, 1995). In

1994 he won a Whiting Writer's Award. He is an associate professor of English at Yale University.

Koestenbaum writes: " '1975' is part of a sequence of short poems, composed in the fall of 1992, and published under the title 'Erotic Collectibles.' I aimed to recapture the vertigo of sexual irresolution. I didn't want to redeem the past but to re-enter it, experimentally, and to give failed, incomplete erotic experience some of the gloss and focus of amorous success.

"Pieces of several separate poems (one of them called 'The Waterbed') found their way into '1975,' the various messy crushes folded together into sleek paradigms."

JOHN KOETHE was born in San Diego in 1945. He did his undergraduate and graduate work at Princeton and Harvard, respectively. His books include *Blue Vents* (Audit/Poetry, 1969); *Domes* (Columbia University Press, 1973), which won the Frank O'Hara Award for Poetry; and *The Late Wisconsin Spring* (Princeton University Press, 1984). His poem "Mistral" received the Bernard F. Connors Award from *The Paris Review* and was included in *The Best American Poetry 1988*. He has received a Guggenheim Fellowship. He is a professor of philosophy at the University of Wisconsin and lives in Milwaukee.

Koethe writes: "I began writing 'Falling Water' in January 1992 after returning from a visit to Frank Lloyd Wright's house and studio in Oak Park, Illinois, and I finished it in November of that year. I had recently moved, and in the course of doing so had begun to develop an interest in Prairie School architecture and the furniture of the Arts and Crafts movement. I found myself intertwining spatial and architectural references with the personal material that constitutes the poem's primary subject matter, and kept doing that in a loose way until the end. The poem turned out to be much longer than I'd anticipated, thanks to my collagistic way of composing by connecting up various lines and fragments that accumulate in the course of writing a poem."

YUSEF KOMUNYAKAA was born in 1947 in Bogalusa, Louisiana. In 1969 and 1970 he served with the U.S. Army in Vietnam. Since 1985, he has taught creative writing and literature at Indiana University. He was the 1992 Holloway Lecturer at the University of California at Berkeley. His latest book, *Neon Vernacular*, was awarded the 1994 Pulitzer Prize and the Kingsley Tufts Award. He also received the 1994 William Faulkner Prize (Université de Rennes). He spent the 1994–95 academic year in Australia.

The Frank O'Hara poem to which "Troubling the Water" alludes is "Personal Poem" (1959), in which Herman Melville, Henry James, Miles Davis, Birdland, the "House of Seagram," and Moriarty's all figure.

Komunyakaa writes: " 'Troubling the Water' is primarily improvisational, stimulated by some gut-level feelings from the Mapplethorpe exhibit four or five years ago in Cincinnati (I remember much heated debate about the photographs). When I viewed the show, it seemed that it was the juxtaposition of images, how the photographs were arranged and displayed, that created much of the visual tension and impact—black and white males and females in a kind of collective double-dare. The taboo and attraction had been aligned through the camera lens. But what was most provocative, for me, was the flower imagery, which suggested sexuality and invited the viewer to be an active participant. My own imagination could create the leaps and do some of the work. This is what I also wanted in my poetry: a collage/montage effect propelled by a certain fluidity. I feel that the desired effect has been accomplished with the three-line-indented stanzas, a structure that invites voluminous data and various departures (inclusion). In fact, it is this same quality of inclusion that makes so much of Frank O'Hara's work so exciting; but I also wanted to address the conspicuous exoticism in some of his poems (especially about blacks). When the human body becomes mere object, this kind of voyeurism dehumanizes us. Until we fully humanize those images in our collective psyche, we are condemned to view many of the images that Mapplethorpe captures as no more than a gelatinous sensationalism."

MAXINE KUMIN was born in Philadelphia, Pennsylvania, in 1925. She has published ten collections of poetry; her fourth, *Up Country*, won the Pulitzer Prize in 1973. Her most recent collection, *Looking for Luck*, won the Poets' Prize in 1994. She is a visiting professor at the University of Miami for the spring of 1995, and has held similar appointments at Brandeis, Columbia, Princeton, and MIT. She lives in New Hampshire.

Of "Getting the Message," Kumin writes: "This poem was commissioned by the Auburn Theological Seminary of New York as part of their sesquicentennial celebration. I undertook the project hesitantly, not at all sure that I could produce a poem on command. My instructions were to expatiate on the verses of Exodus that tell the story of the burning bush. How could an old Jewish agnostic deal with this miracle? In *The Interpreter's One-Volume Commentary on the Bible*, I turned up several fanciful tales that helped me along the way; these then raised Sunday school lessons from my childhood. I had a wonderful time meeting the assignment."

LISA LEWIS was born in Roanoke, Virginia, in 1956. Her first book, *The Unbeliever*, won the Brittingham Prize in 1994 and was published by the University of Wisconsin Press. She is currently writer-in-residence at Rhodes College in Memphis, Tennessee, where she lives with a pit bull terrier named Betty.

Of "Bridget," Lewis writes: "My poem is about girls obeying the law close to them and finding that it conflicts with the law the police enforce. I read a newspaper story about a fourteen-year-old girl shot by the police. Her brother had the idea that a standoff in an empty house and threats of suicide would force his mother to let him live with her again; Bridget was wounded in the cross fire between the police and her brother's defiant friend. Why had she been there at all? No one in the newspaper article asked that question, but it seemed she'd had no purpose of her own. It seemed to me she must have been living up to the 'moral' law that requires women to accompany and help the men they are close to; if those men break the law of the land, the women do, too, though really they've been obedient to the law close at hand and in that sense they are model citizens. The speaker of the poem remembers a similar incident involving herself and male friends in adolescence; she had taken 'their' punishment. Writing this poem made me think that the law is a clumsier instrument than I'd ever guessed. There's a fabric of law applying specifically to women that does not appear in the legal code, and everyone knows about it. Brothers, friends, fathers, husbands, and lovers enforce it, and it informs the morality of accommodation and self-sacrifice that most women practice without getting much credit for it. The coercion is subtler than the law of the land. But it's been around a lot longer, too."

RACHEL LODEN was born in Washington, D.C., in 1948. Her poems have appeared in *New American Writing*, *Seneca Review*, and *Green*

Mountains Review. She is finishing a collection, "Five Minute Ago-raphobic Holidays," which she hopes to publish "sometime this century." She lives in Palo Alto, California, and teaches privately.

Of "My Night with Philip Larkin," Loden writes: "I wrote the poem in the middle of the night after reading photocopied Larkin in the shower (an experiment I recommend to anyone). Discovering my intimacy with this odd, unpleasant, melancholy man suggested that I might make better use of my own peculiarities, and under-scored the eccentric occasion of all poetry. The poem took tradi-tional form, which seemed natural after immersing myself in Larkin."

ROBERT HILL LONG was born in North Carolina in 1952. He is the author of *The Power to Die* (Cleveland State, 1987). He has received a fellowship from the National Endowment for the Arts. He teaches at the University of Oregon in Eugene.

Long writes: " 'Refuge' is one of several short narrative poems I've written in the past few years based on violent acts of political oppression. I regard it as my most *cinematic* poem. The protagonist is an unwilling spectator, forced by events to choose between help-ing the victims or protecting himself. He isn't bad (he doesn't cheer on the killers), but he's no samaritan either. His hands are most comfortable around a book, a camera, a newspaper, a TV remote—not unlike most of my middle-class cohort, who can afford to regard systematic political terror, at home and abroad, from a sub-urban perspective. 'Refuge' was written for them, my neighbors."

JAMES LONGENBACH was born in Plainfield, New Jersey, in 1959. His poems have appeared in *The Paris Review*, *The Southwest Review*, and *The Yale Review*. He is also the author of several books about modern poetry, including *Stone Cottage: Pound, Yeats, and Modernism* and *Wallace Stevens: The Plain Sense of Things*, both pub-lished by Oxford University Press. He and his wife, the novelist Joanna Scott, live in Rochester, New York, where they teach at the University of Rochester. "What You Find in the Woods" is part of a manuscript of poems entitled *Pinnacle Hill*.

Of "What You Find in the Woods," Longenbach writes: "After devoting the better part of a decade to literary criticism, I decided several years ago to return to poetry. I had always continued, how-ever sporadically, to write poems, but this reconfiguration of my writerly life wasn't always easy. And when the work didn't go well, I'd take a walk on Pinnacle Hill, one of those plots of scruffy wilderness that you sometimes find in the middle of suburbia. I've never been much of a nature boy, but this landscape suits me. There's no water, no wildlife, and the ground barely seems strong enough to hold up the trees. If you're a teenager, you come there to drink beer and throw the cans in the ravine. It's hard to imagine why a grown-up would climb the hill at all: I always expect to find something new or strange, but Pinnacle Hill is always the same. The place has no sense of place, and it's consequently one of the most uncanny places I know.

" 'It's not every day that the world arranges itself in a poem,' said Wallace Stevens, but during one morning walk, a hawk settled on a branch about ten feet in front of me. We eyed each other for a few seconds, and then the hawk spread its impossibly large wings and disappeared. I walked home, full of gratitude, and began writing the poem."

GAIL MAZUR was born in Cambridge, Massachusetts, in 1937. She is the author of three books of poetry: *Nightfire* (Godine, 1978), *The Pose of Happiness* (Godine, 1986), and *The Common* (Chicago, 1995). She lives in Provincetown and in Cambridge, where she is director of the Blacksmith House Poetry Center. She teaches a poetry workshop at the Harvard University Extension School.

Of "Fracture Santa Monica," Mazur writes: "I had broken my ankle in Provincetown, which necessitated tedious rehabilitation sessions. At the same time, my bi-coastal life—my children live in Los Angeles—felt 'fractured,' nutty. The voice of my trainer is mine, of course, hectoring, impatient with self-pity in the face of other people's suffering. Ocean Avenue by the Shangri-La Hotel, once serene, gorgeous, and a little funky, is now a tragic stretch of homeless men and women, their sleeping bags and wagons and odd, brave industries a discomfiting backdrop for joggers and strolling retirees. That scene; the charm of the chirping Santa Monica traffic lights; the eucalyptus and coral trees; my dazzled memory of the Canadian Cirque du Soleil's performance on the beach by the pier a year earlier, with Steve Martin, Martin Short, and Dom DeLuise part of an enchanted audience; the fragility and embarrassment one feels after an admittedly minor fracture—these all came together when my mother's old admonition came to me, a rude signal flashing the start of the poem, which came then in a flash."

J. D. MCCLATCHY was born in Bryn Mawr, Pennsylvania, in 1945. He is the author of three books of poems, *Scenes from Another Life* (1981), *Stars Principal* (1986), and *The Rest of the Way* (1990), and a collection of essays, *White Paper* (1989). He has edited many other books, including *Poets on Painters* (1988), and written opera libretti for several composers. He is the editor of *The Yale Review* and lives in Stonington, Connecticut.

Of "My Mammogram," McClatchy writes: "I *did*, a year ago, have a mammogram, but my description of the procedure itself— in the second of the poem's five sonnets—is the only part of the poem that is 'true.' The rest was exaggerated or invented or colored in such a way as to make (or at least this was my intention) the 'experience' seem both more vivid and more substantial, and also perhaps less scary, than it was in fact. The formal distractions of the sonnet form seemed the best way to prompt and control material that could too easily turn sensational or sentimental; the sequence of sonnets as well discourages a plodding or overdetailed narrative. The tone of the poem was hardest to get right. What I tried for was this: a nervous humor about the incongruities at the start that gradually gives way to a darker, more serious meditation."

HEATHER MCHUGH was born to Canadian parents in San Diego in 1948. She was raised in Virginia and educated at Harvard University. For the past decade she has served as Milliman Writer at the University of Washington at Seattle; she is also a core faculty member of the M.F.A. program at Warren Wilson College and a frequent visitor at the University of Iowa Writers' Workshop. Five collections of her poetry have appeared since her first, *Dangers*, was published by Houghton Mifflin in 1977. Her most recent books are *Hinge & Sign: Poems, 1968–1993* (Wesleyan/New England, 1994), which was short-listed for last year's National Book Award in poetry, and *Broken English: Poetry and Partiality* (Wesleyan/New England, 1993).

McHugh writes: "An American reader won't fail to hear, in 'And What Do You Get,' strains of the old standard 'Sixteen Tons'—a coal-mining ballad that conditions the poem's reading. It's up to the reader to bring to the title's tuning the rhyme-chime of 'Another day older and deeper in debt.' Somewhere near the middle of the poem lurk 'eleven tons of hidden work'—that's five tons short of a day's due. A loss always attends language.

"I'm wary of this poem's paronymic program; perhaps I run, in it, the risk of self-parody. No less a wordsmith than Richard Howard has said, 'Poets have a strong weakness for oxymoron.' Mine is his own strong weakness for wordplay. I can only say, in our defense, what Piaget said of children: play is their *work*. Partly I mean gently to mock the working American impulse to cut to the chase—to get there fast with fewer syllables and pounds and years. On the other hand, academic life is laden with wastes of time and burdens of jargon, especially in the two areas I've known best, literary studies and the psycho-social sciences. A poet loving high wit and common sense in equal measure may take a turn for the worse in such departments.

"One of the James brothers said the natural enemy of any science was the professor thereof. The bottom (and tiniest) line in this tirade is reserved for the signature of the meanest expertise—what reduces communication to instrumentality, mind to phone, phone to banker, signature to PIN code. Far from ruing the newest lines of communication, the ones that go mandelbrotting out on optic fibers in the deepest airwaves, and far from ignoring the old direct leap of meanings, straight to sense from synapse, I hope the poem argues for a receptivity narrowed neither by jargon-overload nor by closed-mindedness (born of fear or habit or mere self-interest). Using a synthesizer to imitate a violin is a waste of an opportunity. Each shift of form reveals a source of energy. Not to discover it is to wind up carrying the same old coals to Newcastle."

SUSAN MUSGRAVE was born in Santa Cruz, California, in 1951. She was raised on Vancouver Island in British Columbia, Canada, and has spent extended periods of time in Ireland, England, the Queen Charlotte Islands, Panama, and Colombia. Her books of poetry include *Forcing the Narcissus* (McClelland and Stewart, 1994) and *The Embalmer's Art: Poems New and Selected* (Exile Editions, 1991). *Musgrave Landing: Musings on the Writing Life* appeared in 1994 (Stoddart). Her short fiction has recently appeared (or is soon to appear) in *Fever: Sensual Stories by Women Writers* (Harcourt, Brace, 1994) and *Best American Erotica 1995* (Simon & Schuster). She received the University of Toronto's Presidential Writer-in-Residence

Fellowship in 1995. She and her husband live near Sidney, British Columbia.

Of "Exchange of Fire," Musgrave writes: "This poem evolved from the idea of adultery in the '90s, 'safe' adultery, adultery confined to the imagination. Remember what it feels like when another person touches you, seemingly innocently, and you feel a spark, an undeniable bolt of sexual lightning, connecting the two of you, with terrible consequences if you choose to let your feelings be known. In 'Exchange of Fire' I wanted to show what could happen when that spark, which has to be repressed because of the friendships and marriages at stake, goes its own way, burning out of control."

CHARLES NORTH was born in New York City in 1941. An active musician in his youth, he played clarinet with his first orchestra at the age of thirteen and spent summers at the music program in Interlochen, Michigan. He received degrees from Tufts University and Columbia University and briefly attended Harvard Law School. He is the author of seven collections of poetry, most recently *The Year of the Olive Oil* (Hanging Loose, 1989) and the forthcoming *Shooting for Line: New and Selected Poems* (Sun & Moon). With James Schuyler he edited *Broadway: A Poets and Painters Anthology* (Swollen Magpie, 1979) and *Broadway 2* (Hanging Loose, 1989). He is one of the editors of *The Green Lake Is Awake: Selected Poems by Joseph Ceravolo*. North is poet-in-residence at Pace University.

North writes: " 'Shooting for Line' is an ode to zeugma, or perhaps syllepsis, a two-tone rhetorical device I fell in love with years ago in a class in eighteenth-century English literature with Sylvan Barnet: 'Or stain her honour, or her new brocade' (Pope). 'Shooting for Line' is a printer's phrase referring to a line negative as opposed to halftone reproduction."

GEOFFREY O'BRIEN was born in New York City in 1948. He is the author of two books of poetry, *A Book of Maps* (1989) and *The Hudson Mystery* (1994), both published by Red Dust, and three prose works, *The Phantom Empire* (Norton, 1993), *Dream Time: Chapters from the Sixties* (Viking Penguin, 1988), and *Hardboiled America* (Van Nostrand Reinhold, 1981). His criticism has appeared frequently in *The New York Review of Books* and *Voice Literary*

Supplement. He edited *The Reader's Catalog*, which appeared in 1989. He lives in New York City, where he is the executive editor of the Library of America.

Of "The Interior Prisoner," O'Brien writes: "The poem began to write itself in a dream that had something to do with sequestration. A voice emanated from a cell; a poem had to be translated from another language, a kind of dream-Spanish flavored by blurred recollections of Calderon and Machado. Outside the room where I was sleeping it was winter in Essex, just before Christmas, in a neighborhood whose earlier religious turmoil I had just read about in Charles Dickens's *Barnaby Rudge*.

"On waking, and for a period of two weeks thereafter, the sections continued to make their way forward, rooted always in a meditation on the unseen and foreign writer in that cell back there. The writer was characterized solely by what he or she would have, or could have, written—not by any other trait or biographical fact, beyond the reclusion (whether voluntary or otherwise) indicated by the poem's title. For that reason I decided to retain the cryptic and possibly unnecessary subtitle; it seemed important to allude to the elusive yet oddly empathetic author without whose imagined existence the poem would not have come to be at all."

JACQUELINE OSHEROW was born in 1956. Her two books, *Conversations with Survivors* (1994) and *Looking for Angels in New York* (1988), were published in the University of Georgia Press Contemporary Poets Series. The title poem of her most recent book was awarded the John Masefield Memorial Award by the Poetry Society of America in 1993. She has also received a grant from the Ingram Merrill Foundation. She teaches English and American literature as well as creative writing at the University of Utah. She lives in Salt Lake City.

Osherow writes: "I'm a little hesitant to say anything about 'Late Night Tête-à-Tête with a Moon in Transit'; a poem this long ought to be able to explain itself. But I thought I might say something about the circumstances of its writing, which began in my second month of pregnancy with my third daughter. Like pregnancy, the poem dragged on and on. It became the poem I was endlessly working on, throwing every memory, every obsession, into it, and enjoying the delusion that all could be held together by a peculiar paste of terza rima and the moon. As my due date drew nearer, I kept thinking that I had to finish the poem before the baby was born or I would thoroughly lose whatever hold on it I had. But I didn't feel well at all and couldn't concentrate.

"The baby was born and ordinarily I wouldn't have cared about the poem. But a reading had been scheduled to take place a month after her birth and I hated the idea of not reading what I'd been working on for all that time. I started to play around with lines in my head while she was nursing, and, as she slept on my shoulder, I typed the rest of the poem one-handed. So the last quarter? fifth? of the poem has within it, for me at least, that fleeting instant when a newborn's weight is indistinguishable from your own, and the occasional interruption of a tiny sigh."

MOLLY PEACOCK was born in Buffalo, New York, in 1947, and lives both in London, Ontario, Canada, and New York City. She is the author of four books, including *Original Love* (Norton, 1995) and *Take Heart* (Vintage, 1989). Her poems have appeared in *The New Yorker*, *The Paris Review*, *The Nation*, *The New Republic*, and *Poetry*. She was president of the Poetry Society of America from 1989 until 1994. She teaches privately on a one-on-one basis throughout North America.

Of "Have You Ever Faked an Orgasm?" Peacock writes: "One of the pleasures of being a poet at the end of the twentieth century is writing about a subject that has existed in its richness since the beginning of the species but has until now been little found in literature: female sexuality. This sequence of five poems about female sexuality depicts psychological experiences that are dangerously unclassifiable because they are complex and require several different responses at once. (The gamble each poem takes is that there are other women out there who feel as I do.) I wrote these poems after the breakup of a long relationship, when I felt it was possible that I would never again feel sexually comfortable with another person. The awkwardness of my early sexuality and of my fantasies and observations surfaced at this time, and I tapped into them as I wrote. In these five poems I am deliberately on the furthest edge of social acceptability. They all ask, How far should art go? And all answer, I hope, that we must reveal to have the experience of revelation."

CARL PHILLIPS was born in 1959 and grew up on air force bases. A classics major at Harvard, he taught high school Latin for nearly a decade. His first book of poems, *In the Blood* (Northeastern University Press), won the 1992 Samuel French Morse Poetry Prize. A second volume will appear from Graywolf Press in the fall of 1995. He currently lives in St. Louis, Missouri, where he is an assistant professor at Washington University.

Of "Toys," Phillips writes: "As a former student and teacher of Greek and Latin, I continue to be intrigued at the ways in which the classical world—at least to *my* eye—insists on maintaining some foothold in the contemporary one. This was the case in Provincetown a couple of summers ago when for the first time I stumbled upon a display of sex toys, as they're sometimes called. This encounter recalled for me a story I'd heard years earlier from a professor in Rome—true?—regarding the storage of members removed from the city's statues. The thoughts that followed my connecting of these two separate events resulted in the poem."

MARIE PONSOT was born in New York City in 1921. She worked briefly at UNESCO in Paris; she then worked as a translator for ten years and a teacher for twenty-six. Her translations include *Tales of La Fontaine* (Signet Classics, 1966). She has taught at Queens College, the City University of New York, Cooper Union, the University of Houston, and Beijing United University. Her book on the teaching of writing, *Beat Not the Poor Desk* (Heinemann, 1982), written in collaboration with Rosemary Deen, won the MLA Shaughnessy Medal. She lists her seven children as major awards.

Of "Old Mama Saturday," Ponsot writes: "It was composed with the boisterous elation that springs from making a definitive choice (in this case, between two goods: to stay/to change). Such elation, the poem finds, can outface the imps of anxiety. Puns, plain rhymes, and short-breath lines aim at keeping the imps in their place, skipping, hip-hop. The speaker has the privilege of being old.

"The field of 'old' is distorted by bad maps, scribbled with stiff guesses and false claims. So, being old—being female and old and liking it—I need to work without maps to see the world from that verge. I write hoping to grow up through a language that is poetry, is not false, and does no harm."

BIN RAMKE was born in Port Neches, Texas, in 1947. He is the author of five books of poetry, including *Massacre of the Innocents* (Iowa, 1995), *The Erotic Light of Gardens* (Wesleyan, 1989), and *The Language Student* (LSU, 1986). He has been editing the Contemporary Poetry Series of the University of Georgia Press for the past ten years. He is now the editor of the *Denver Quarterly* and directs the creative writing program at the University of Denver.

Ramke writes: " 'How Light Is Spent' steals shamelessly from Milton, because there is no shame (see Prometheus) when one steals from gods.

"Two of my uncles were, in fact, blind. One was a jazz musician with whom my rather saintly aunt could not, finally, live. The other earned his Ph.D. in history during the Depression in spite of his family's rural poverty. And yet my most vivid memory of either man's life was of their brothers at dinner telling them what was on their plates by reference to the face of the clock.

"The danger in playing poetically against a monument such as Sonnet XIX is that a reader will be reminded of the grandeur of the original. This is to be recommended. Perhaps in my own defense I can ask, 'Doth God exact day-labour, light deny'd?' I write only according to my gifts, but I admire admirably."

KATRINA ROBERTS was born in Red Bank, New Jersey, in 1965. She has been a resident at the MacDowell Colony, and has received two Garrison Medals in poetry, a Briggs Literary Traveling Fellowship, and a grant from the St. Botolph Foundation. She lives in Cambridge, Massachusetts, and teaches at the Harvard Extension School and Boston University.

Of "How Late Desire Looks," Roberts writes: "Mine is an island mentality: salt water as blood, a body of cliff and scrub, and a mind for mist and wind. I feel at home in the pulsing city as well, though each of the three places I had lived in just prior to moving to New Hampshire—where I wrote the poem—was in its way a remote island: an egg of land in the Atlantic off France, a sixteenth-century walled-in Tuscan village, and Iowa City. For one who takes flight like a gypsy, toting what feels essential on her back, there is a kind of longing made concrete in the perfume and riot of somebody's cultivated summer garden. Wings and roots. The trick is to have both. Is anything ever 'not already caught'? Probably not. A love poem as all are, and a revolt—I wrote it in a burst, as consolation for what could not exist elsewhere. The act of disclosure was aggressive, *yes*, but in enacting the fragment, I discovered an elegance that I might have missed in the actual living—a choreography of petals and illusory plumage, the dancing of glancing eyes, the breaths insucked after an afternoon spent climbing mountain trails on bikes. I have coaxed facts slightly to breathe life into that bubble where we two still hover like others frozen never to kiss. Was there more to the story? Of course."

MICHAEL J. ROSEN was born in Columbus, Ohio, in 1954. He is the author of a poetry collection, *A Drink at the Mirage* (Princeton University Press, 1985), as well as several children's books, most recently *Bonesy and Isabel* and *A School for Pompey Walker* (both Harcourt, Brace, 1995). He has edited four anthologies of stories to benefit animal welfare efforts through a granting program he began in 1990; *Dog People, Portraits of Canine Companionship* has just been released from Artisan. He has also created three anthologies to benefit Share Our Strength's fight against hunger. He continues to live in Columbus, where he has been literary director of the Thurber House since its inception in 1982.

Of "The Night Before His Parents' First Trip to Europe His Mother Writes a Letter 'To Our Children,'" Rosen writes: "My parents have never been great readers, and I was not brought up to think of poetry as a significant source of pleasure. They encouraged me nonetheless when I began writing the stuff in junior high school. When I left medical school for the sake of poetry, they were able to accommodate what was clearly a curious and risky choice—to their minds and somewhat to my own.

"The idea of having a poet for a son has grown on them. Whenever a poem of mine appears in a general magazine, they make the rounds of local newsstands in order to buy copies for relatives.

"The occasion for this poem is proclaimed in its title. What preoccupied me for days was imagining the sentences a mother would write in a letter for her children to read upon the news of her (and her husband's) death. What those words might have been, I couldn't imagine.

"Around the time I wrote this poem, I finished another involving 'the poet/son.' Its title: 'His Father Phones with an Idea for a Poem.'"

KAY RYAN was born in California in 1945, and grew up in the small towns of the San Joaquin Valley and the Mojave Desert. She studied at the Los Angeles and Irvine campuses of the University of California. Since 1971 she has lived in Marin County and has made her living teaching basic language skills part-time at the College of Marin and for some years at San Quentin Prison. She has published two books of poetry, *Flamingo Watching* (1994) and *Strangely Marked Metal* (1985), both from Copper Beech Press. She is a recent recipient of an Ingram Merrill award.

Of "Outsider Art," Ryan writes: "I had been looking at a big handsome book of American primitive art, and it dawned gradually and disagreeably upon me that I didn't like it. The work of these isolates felt urgent and obsessed, squeezing me out. I almost never describe actual things in poems and the fact that I have here just goes to show how invaded I felt by this stuff. I don't even want to think about whether they're my spiritual cousins."

MARY JO SALTER was born in Grand Rapids, Michigan, in 1954, and grew up mostly in Baltimore. A graduate of Harvard University and of Cambridge, she has worked as a staff editor at *The Atlantic Monthly* and as poetry editor of *The New Republic*. Since 1984 she has been a lecturer in English at Mount Holyoke College. Her first collection of poems, *Henry Purcell in Japan* (Knopf, 1985), was followed by *Unfinished Painting* (Knopf, 1989), which won the Lamont Prize, and *Sunday Skaters* (Knopf, 1994). She has also published a children's book, *The Moon Comes Home* (Knopf, 1989). With her husband, Brad Leithauser, she has lived for extended periods abroad in Japan, England, Italy, Iceland, and most recently France, where she was a Guggenheim Fellow in 1993.

Of "The Age of Reason," Salter writes: "I suppose what distinguishes this little poem from most I write is that it relies on symbols more than on metaphors and similes. My child's birthday is an occasion to celebrate her attaining 'the age of reason'—a milestone most often misrecognized, paradoxically, by people of faith. That irony is complicated by my parents' decision, implied in the poem, to leave Catholicism for Unitarianism, long before I knew how to apply reason to understanding the difference. More ironies lodge themselves in symbols—like the heavenly reward of the devil's food birthday cake, the thing waited for after a lifetime (it seems) of tedium; the popped balloon of disillusionment; and the candles, which are, depending on how you look at them, either festive or a threat of hellfire. If the poem succeeds at its graver level, it's because I tried to keep it light—or to have my cake and eat it, too."

TONY SANDERS was born in New York City in 1957. His poems have appeared in *The Paris Review*, *Grand Street*, and *The Gettysburg Review*. His first collection, *Partial Eclipse* (University of North Texas Press, 1994), won the Vassar Miller Prize. He teaches at Fairfield University.

Of "Transit Authority," Sanders writes: "The poem has some origin in an experience I had on a deteriorating expressway. Stuck in a traffic jam with the fuel gauge on empty, I elected to exit in reverse via a crowded on-ramp to find the nearest gas station. The landscape provided the foundation for the overall conceit."

STEPHEN SANDY was born in Minneapolis, Minnesota, in 1938. He is the author of six volumes of poetry, including *Thanksgiving Over the Water* (1994), *Man in Open Air* (1988), and *Riding to Greylock* (1983), all from Knopf, and *Roofs* (1971) and *Stresses in the Peaceable Kingdom* (1967) from Houghton Mifflin. He has held a Fulbright Lectureship in Japan at the University of Tokyo. He is also the author of *The Raveling of the Novel* (Arno Press, 1981), a study of eighteenth- and nineteenth-century English fiction, and *A Cloak for Hercules* (Johns Hopkins University Press, 1995), a translation of Seneca's *Hercules Oetaeus*. He has taught at Bennington College for many years and was the McGee Professor of Writing at Davidson College in 1994.

Of "Threads," Sandy writes: "These poems were not written in the confessional mode and are only tangentially about growing up in the rag trade, as I did; historicity, Auden wrote, does not ensure relevance. The operation of a childhood memory upon the adult self provoked these sonnets.

"In particular the incandescent image of a serial number, tattooed on the forearm of a refugee from Auschwitz, remained vibrant, the sole immediate contact with the Holocaust a midwestern boy had growing up in Sam Kahn's pattern-making room, much against the pattern maker's will; thence to the cutting tables. Her forearm gleams across the years blazoning its code of cruelty and force. But then it was only a weird, intriguing mystery that no one would talk about; that set her life apart. It placed her in a nimbus of the exotic that only dissipated after years to show the cess of violence and oppression, and our banal accommodation of outrage and despair."

GRACE SCHULMAN was born in New York City in 1935. Her poetry collections include *Burn Down the Icons* (Princeton University Press, 1976), *Hemispheres* (Sheep Meadow Press, 1984), and *For That Day Only* (Sheep Meadow Press, 1994). She is also the author of a critical study, *Marianne Moore: The Poetry of Engagement* (University of Illinois Press). She received her M.A. and Ph.D. from New York University and is a professor of English at Baruch College, City University of New York. She is poetry editor of *The Nation*, a position she has held since 1972, and was the director of the Poetry Center at the 92nd Street YM-YWHA, New York City, from 1974 to 1984.

Of "The Present Perfect," Schulman writes: "This is a meditation on a long marriage that survived early trials related to childlessness. The ironies seemed endless: freedom from restriction—on travel, privacy, conversation—could also deprive life of its vitality. Reading great books, for which there was leisure, clarified the truth that art transcends life. And yet there were those archetypal reminders of progeny: the biblical blessings ('that thou and thy seed may live'); and the Kaddish—in the Jewish tradition, a prayer of mourning once thought of as the reciter's plea to liberate his dead parent's soul.

"Still, my poem turned to praise. I had been reading one of Wyatt's sonnets, in which love's changes are presented in heightened moments, and cast in the present tense. In contrast I thought of my own loyalties as existing in 'the present perfect tense'—not 'I love' but 'I have loved.' At the same time, I looked to Wyatt's poems for the compelling way he uses ironies that contend with form. I wrote 'The Present Perfect' as a love poem to my husband, Jerome.

"He is a scientist whose wonder at the mystery of living things expresses a faith beyond the secular. Originally the poem was titled 'And Yet.' It seems to contradict itself at every turn except one: 'We have been married thirty-four years,' set in the present perfect, the tense of emotional fixity.'"

ROBYN SELMAN was born in New York City in 1959. Her first book of poems, *Directions to My House*, was published in 1995 by the University of Pittsburgh Press.

Selman writes: " 'Avec Amour' was written in the spring of

1993, after the mastectomy surgery of someone very close to me. This friend was one of the many women I have known who've been victims of breast cancer—among them, my own mother and stepmother. I meant the poem to show a progression of my consciousness—social, sexual, political—and finally, ending with my friend's illness, to merge the inner and outer, the manifold meanings of the word *war* in this century.

"The poem was revised a zillion times. I felt ambivalent about focusing on my friend's cancer—as I do whenever I write a narrative poem that is based on my experience with other people. And though I leave out names, or change them, their presence is central to the poem. Somehow I will never be entirely comfortable with that arrangement. And so you see that the details in the sequence are largely about myself. Other figures are more lightly sketched—not out of fear of identifying them, but out of a respect I feel is due to people who will, in one way or another, tell their own stories in their own language—be it written, painted, by act, or even by silence."

ALAN SHAPIRO was born in Boston in 1952. He received his B.A. from Brandeis University in 1974. He has published four books of poetry: *After the Digging* (Elpenor Books, 1981), *The Courtesy* (University of Chicago Press, 1983), *Happy Hour* (Chicago, 1987), and *Covenant* (Chicago, 1991). A new book of poems, *Mixed Company*, is forthcoming from Chicago in 1996. A book of essays, *In Praise of the Impure: Poetry and the Ethical Imagination*, was published in 1993 by TriQuarterly Books. He has received fellowships from the National Endowment for the Arts and the Guggenheim Foundation, and was the recipient of a Lila Wallace–Reader's Digest Writer's Award in 1991. In the fall of 1995, he became a professor of English and creative writing at the University of North Carolina in Chapel Hill.

Shapiro writes: "The thirteen-year-old boy in 'Manufacturing' is trying to understand his emerging sexuality by decoding the sexual assumptions implicit in the language he overhears his father and uncle using."

REGINALD SHEPHERD was born in New York City in 1963 and raised in the housing projects and tenements in the Bronx. He received his B.A. from Bennington College in 1988 and the M.F.A. from both Brown University (1991) and the University of Iowa (1993). His book *Some Are Drowning* (Pittsburgh) was chosen by Carolyn Forché for the 1993 Associated Writing Programs' Award Series in Poetry. His second collection, *Angel, Interrupted*, will appear from Pittsburgh in 1996. He received a fellowship in poetry from the National Endowment for the Arts in 1995. He lives in Chicago and teaches at Northern Illinois University in DeKalb.

Shepherd writes: " 'Brotherhood' is a rather odd poem for me. It marked a threshold of sorts. I wrote the first version soon after returning to college after three years of underpaid menial labor. Over the course of those three years, I found my carefully cultivated interiority, my 'self' (as an 'artist,' as an 'intellectual'), to be irrelevant to the life (the *soi-disant* 'real world' about which I had been admonished so frequently) that, if not mine, certainly had *me* firmly in its grasp, and to whose demands and requests I found myself inexorably surrendering. This poem was one of my first attempts to grapple, however mediately, with this life (and my position as its *subject* in both senses) as it was, rather than as it might (in the realm of fantasmatic compensation) be made to appear. The poem was also, not to be paradoxical, one of my first literary attempts to explore the made (and thus contingent) character of the social and material world, usually taken as given and fixed. My work up to then had consisted of my attempts to escape my life for and by means of the world of art: to flee anywhere out of this world, in Baudelaire's words. I wanted to make beautiful things about things everyone agreed were beautiful, because beauty would both redress and justify my life, and I couldn't imagine any other kind of beauty than the tautological. 'Brotherhood' was one of my first poems to investigate rather than simply illustrate that desire, to interrogate rather than simply long for the beautiful. My friend Jenny Mueller once told me she thought much of my work constituted an argument between beauty and justice: I hope that in this poem justice argues beauty at least to a stalemate.

"I'd like to dedicate this poem to Alvin Feinman, who as my thesis tutor at Bennington College saw possibilities in 'Brotherhood,' and in my work as a whole, of which I had remained largely unaware until his prompting. I hope some of those promised finer revelations have come to pass."

ANGELA SORBY was born in Seattle, Washington, in 1965. She studied with the late Nelson Bentley at the University of Washington, and is currently completing a Ph.D. in English at the University of Chicago. She has received a Fisk Poetry Prize, a fellowship from the Centrum Foundation, and a 1994 "Discovery"/*The Nation* prize. She serves as poetry editor of the *Chicago Review*, where she recently edited a special issue on poetry and mass culture.

Sorby writes: " 'Museum Piece' is about a real person, although the name has been changed and the wedding scene is a fictional frame. Susan's real-life analogue did not grow into a conventional suburban bride; in fact, she ran away to Europe halfway through high school, and is currently teaching English in northern Norway, where Sami people sell reindeer kabobs on the street. But the poem is true insofar as it honors the intense and yet ephemeral quality of adolescent friendship, and acknowledges that the notes young girls pass to one another are truly love notes."

LAUREL TRIVELPIECE was born in Nebraska in 1926. She accompanied her family to California as part of the Okie tide. Working a variety of jobs (starting with fruit picking), she graduated from the University of California at Berkeley in 1948 and worked in advertising in San Francisco and New York. When her children were school-age, she was able to begin her own writing. She is the author of four books for young adults: *During Water Peaches* (Lippincott, 1977), *In Love and In Trouble* (Pocket, 1981), *Trying Not to Love You* (Pocket, 1985), and *Just a Little Bit Lost* (Scholastic, 1988). Her two books of poetry are *Legless in Flight* (Woolmer/Brotherson, 1978) and *Blue Holes* (Alice James Books, 1987). *Triad*, a novel, appeared in 1980 (Pocket).

Of "The Nursery," Trivelpiece writes: "Actually, I never got to the hospital in time to see the new baby in the nursery with all the others, but his birth started the wheel turning."

PAUL VIOLI was born in New York City in 1944. He is the author of seven books of poetry, including *The Curious Builder* (1993) and *Likewise* (1988), both from Hanging Loose Press, and *Splurge* (1981) and *Harmatan* (1977), from SUN Press. He has received poetry fellowships twice from the National Endowment for the Arts. He has worked as managing editor of *Architectural Forum*, on special projects for Universal Limited Art Editions, and as a teacher at various colleges and universities. He is currently collaborating with printmakers Anthony Davies and Dale Devereux Barker.

Of "Scatter," Violi writes: "I'd like to make a statement about this poem but for all my high- and lowfalutin attempts, I can't get beyond the instant that set it off. One windy April day I saw two white-haired sisters, very small and thin, in long dresses, outside their ramshackle colonial, wielding long pruning saws and shears. They could hardly stand in that gale, let alone snip the overgrown lilacs waving beyond their reach, but like a crew trimming sail after a spell in the doldrums, they were loving every minute of it. Their exhilaration was infectious. Whatever its overall effect, the poem began as an extension of that instant. Hence, the increasingly longer sentences, the cataloguing run amok—I was trying to get the sense if not the music of affirmation the image of those two old ladies generated on the kind of windy day that scatters and gathers things simultaneously."

ARTHUR VOGELSANG was born in Baltimore, Maryland, in 1942. He attended the University of Maryland, Johns Hopkins University, and the University of Iowa. His books of poetry are *A Planet* (Holt, 1983), *Twentieth Century Women* (University of Georgia Press, 1988), and the forthcoming *Cities and Towns*. He has been an editor of *The American Poetry Review* since 1973.

Vogelsang writes: " 'The Nose, the Grand Canyon, and the Sixties' began when I tried to write three poems as quickly as I could, with speed the paramount consideration. I didn't know which of the subjects I loved the most. Thereupon immediately I planned to put them together. In the poem I hope the three things take qualities from each other, as they do not in real life, where space is space like this is this, plans are foolish, time moves instantaneously or not at all, and love can't move big objects."

DAVID WAGONER was born in Massillon, Ohio, in 1926, and grew up in Whiting, Indiana. He has taught English at DePauw University, Penn State, and the University of Washington, where he is a professor. He was the editor of the Princeton University Poetry Series from 1978 to 1981. His thirteen books include *Collected Poems* (Indiana University Press, 1976) and *Through the Forest: New and Selected Poems, 1977–1987* (Atlantic Monthly Press, 1987). He is also the author of many novels and the editor of *Straw for the Fire:*

From the Notebooks of Theodore Roethke, 1943–1963 (Doubleday, 1972). A chancellor of the Academy of American Poets, he has been the editor of *Poetry Northwest* since 1966.

Of "Walt Whitman Bathing," Wagoner writes: "Like many other writers, I've changed my mind several times about Walt Whitman and his poetry, my admiration having been joined at times by an almost equal amount of exasperation. Until this poem, I had never written anything about him, not even in notes to myself. But when I finally got around to reading a good biography, I was struck very strongly by some of his behavior after he'd suffered a stroke, and felt such sympathy and empathy with how he acted, I wrote 'Walt Whitman Bathing' almost at ease, with very little revision, feeling something like I imagine he felt then."

CHARLES H. WEBB was born in Philadelphia in 1952, and grew up in Houston, Texas. Educated at Rice University, the University of Washington, and the University of Southern California, he made his living as a rock singer/guitarist for twelve years, and is currently professor of English at California State University, Long Beach, and a licensed psychotherapist. His most recent books of poetry include, in limited editions, *A Weeb for All Seasons* (Applezaba, 1992) and *Everyday Outrages* (Red Wind, 1989). He has also published a novel, *The Wilderness Effect* (Chatto and Windus, 1982), and edited *Stand Up Poetry: The Anthology* (University Press, CSU Long Beach, 1994).

Of "The Shape of History," Webb writes: "As a rule, I'm not a fan of 'shaped' poems. A poem shaped as interlocking male and female symbols I once mistook for a chicken perched on a commode. (That's a true story.) 'The Shape of History,' though, was visually conceived. I pictured an infinitely long first line tapering to that infinitely tiny, infinitely dense point into which all the mass in the universe was gathered, so they say, before the Big Bang.

"The poem was sparked as I was reading a thick newspaper, and reflecting on how briefly even 'big' stories stay big. This made me think of humankind's normal and necessary self-involvement: our frequent sense that what's happening to us is more important than anything that has ever happened before. All of this struck me as simultaneously funny and sad, true and false, trivial and profound—contradictions I tried to embody in the tone of the poem.

"My computer helped a lot with revision. Without my faithful

Mac and the 'Center' command, I might not have persisted with my tornado, or might still be rearranging lines today."

ED WEBSTER was born in Palo Alto, California, in 1958. He writes, "Although I've lived all over the country, I prefer to call Philadelphia home. My seemingly circuitous education began at Tulane University, and it includes—happily—several years working variously as a carpenter and as a musician." He began his graduate studies at Temple University and is currently a Ph.D. candidate at the University of Cincinnati, where he was the 1991–92 Elliston Poetry Fellow.

Of "San Joaquin Valley Poems: 1969," Webster writes: "In 1969 I was living at the Naval Air Station in Lemoore, California, in the San Joaquin Valley. My father was a naval aviator, stationed there with an A-4 squadron. That year his squadron was assigned to the aircraft carrier *Oriskany* and sent to Vietnam.

"I started first versions of these poems five years ago. I wanted to say something about what I remembered of the valley: what it was like to live there, waiting for my father to return. But the poems are also about *remembering* the valley, about considering that time, now, with an understanding not available to me then.

"These poems are for my parents, Edward and Paula Massie Webster."

DAVID WOJAHN was born in St. Paul, Minnesota, in 1953. He is the author of four collections of poetry: *Icehouse Lights* (Yale, 1982), *Glassworks* (Pittsburgh, 1987), *Mystery Train* (Pittsburgh, 1990), and *Late Empire* (Pittsburgh, 1994). He has received fellowships from the National Endowment for the Arts, the Fine Arts Work Center in Provincetown, and the Illinois Council for the Arts. He teaches in the creative writing program at Indiana University and in the M.F.A. program at Vermont College. He lives in Chicago.

Of "Homage to Ryszard Kapuściński," Wojahn writes: "Kapuściński is a Polish journalist who, over the course of a very long career, has reported on some thirty revolutions, and probably an equal number of civil wars and related conflicts—some of them rather obscure to Westerners—ranging from Ethiopia after the fall of Haile Selassie to the Angolan civil war of the 1970s. Kapuściński has the soul of a poet, and his reports of these events are an astonishing combination of sharply drawn (and often grotesque) vignettes and a deeply tragic sense of history. It's the sweep and wry intelligence of his writing, its cinematic pacing, that attracts me; at times, his approach reminds me of poets such as Robert Lowell and of filmmakers such as Bernardo Bertolucci. 'Homage to Ryszard Kapuściński' draws on material from several of his books, including *The Emperor*, *The Soccer War*, and *Another Day of Life*. Some of the details are lifted directly from Kapuściński, while some are my own reconstructions of public events. Each section is a skewed sort of sonnet, as this form seemed the best way to replicate the jittery lyricality of Kapuściński's reportage."

JAY WRIGHT was born in Albuquerque, New Mexico, in "1934 or 1935." He is a poet and playwright whose publications include *The Homecoming Singer* (Corinth Books, 1971), *Soothsayers and Omens* (Seven Woods Press, 1976), *Dimensions of History* (Kayak Books, 1976), *The Double Invention of Komo* (Texas, 1980), *Explications/ Interpretations* (Kentucky, 1984), *Selected Poems* (Princeton, 1987), *Elaine's Book* (University Press of Virginia, 1988), and *Boleros* (Princeton, 1991). He lives in New Hampshire.

STEPHEN YENSER was born in 1941 in Wichita, Kansas. He is a professor of English at U.C.L.A., where he has received the Harvey L. Eby Award for the Art of Teaching. He has also taught in France and Greece on Fulbright grants and in Iraq. He is the author of *Circle to Circle: The Poetry of Robert Lowell* (University of California Press, 1975) and *The Consuming Myth: The Work of James Merrill* (Harvard University Press, 1987). *The Fire in All Things* (Louisiana State University Press, 1993) won the Walt Whitman Award from the Academy of American Poets. "Blue Guide" received the Bernard F. Connors Prize from *The Paris Review*.

Of "Blue Guide," Yenser writes: "The epigraph is from 'The End of March,' and indeed 'Blue Guide' is in large part, if not an elegy, a tribute to Elizabeth Bishop, whose travel poems have helped us all to see both places and poetry anew. The principal town on an Aegean island is often called Chóra (the name means 'town' today but meant something different to Plato); 'Kykládes' transliterates the name of the group of islands frequently called in English the Cyclades; and 'trigoniá' are doves. The Graeae and the Cyclopes will be familiar to those with a smattering of Greek mythology."

MAGAZINES WHERE THE POEMS
WERE FIRST PUBLISHED

American Poetry Review, eds. Stephen Berg, David Bonanno, and Arthur Vogelsang. 1721 Walnut Street, Philadelphia, Pa. 19103.

The American Voice, ed. Frederick Smock. The Kentucky Foundation for Women, Inc., 332 West Broadway, Louisville, Ky. 40202.

The Antioch Review, poetry ed. David St. John. P.O. Box 148, Antioch, Ohio 45387.

apex of the M, eds. Lew Daly, Alan Gilbert, Kristin Prevallet, Pam Rehm. P.O. Box 247, Buffalo, N.Y. 14213–0247.

The Atlantic Monthly, ed. Peter Davison. 745 Boylston Street, Boston, Mass. 02116.

B City, ed. Connie Deanovich. 517 North Fourth Street, DeKalb, Ill. 60115.

Boston Phoenix, poetry ed. Lloyd Schwartz. 126 Brookline Ave., Boston, Mass. 02215.

Boulevard, ed. Richard Burgin. P.O. Box 30386. Philadelphia, Pa. 19103.

Callaloo, ed. Charles H. Rowell. University of Virginia, Department of English, Wilson Hall, Charlottesville, Va. 22903.

Chelsea, ed. Richard Foerster. Box 773, Cooper Station, New York, N.Y. 10276–0773.

Colorado Review, poetry ed. Jorie Graham. 359 Eddy/Department of English, Colorado State University, Fort Collins, Colo. 80523.

Field, eds. Stuart Friebert and David Young. Rice Hall, Oberlin College, Oberlin, Ohio 44074.

The Georgia Review, ed. Stanley Lindberg. University of Georgia, Athens, Ga. 30602.

The Gettysburg Review, ed. Peter Stitt. Gettysburg College, Gettysburg, Pa. 17325–1491.

Hambone, ed. Nathaniel Mackey. 134 Hunolt Street, Santa Cruz, Calif. 95060.

Hanging Loose, eds. Robert Hershon, Dick Lourie, Mark Pawlak, and Ron Schreiber. 231 Wyckoff Street, Brooklyn, N.Y. 11217.

Harvard Magazine, poetry ed. Liam Rector. 7 Ware Street, Cambridge, Mass. 02138.

Harvard Review, ed. Stratis Haviaris. Poetry Room, Harvard College Library, Cambridge, Mass. 02138.

The Iowa Review, ed. David Hamilton. 308 EPB, University of Iowa, Iowa City, Iowa 52242.

Kansas Quarterly, ed. Ben Nyberg. Department of English, Dennison Hall, Kansas State University, Manhattan, Kan. 66506–0703.

Manoa, eds. Robert Shapard and Frank Stewart. English Department, University of Hawaii, Honolulu, Hawaii 96822.

The Massachusetts Review, eds. Jules Chametzky, Mary Heath, Paul Jenkins. Memorial Hall, U. of Massachusetts, Amherst, Mass. 01003.

Michigan Quarterly Review, ed. Laurence Goldstein. University of Michigan, 3032 Rackham Building, Ann Arbor, Mich. 48109–1070.

The Nation, poetry ed. Grace Schulman. 72 Fifth Avenue, New York, N.Y. 10011.

New American Writing, eds. Maxine Chernoff and Paul Hoover. 2920 West Pratt, Chicago, Ill. 60645.

The New Republic, poetry ed. Mark Strand. 1220 19th Street, NW. Washington, D.C. 20036.

The New Yorker, poetry ed. Alice Quinn. 20 West 43rd Street, New York, N.Y. 10036.

Nimrod, ed. Francine Ringold. Arts & Humanities Council of Tulsa, 2210 S. Main St., Tulsa, Okla. 74114.

North American Review, poetry ed. Peter Cooley. University of Northern Iowa, 1227 W. 27th St., Cedar Falls, Iowa 50614–0516.

Painted Bride Quarterly, ed. Teresa Leo. 230 Vine Street, Philadelphia, Pa. 19106.

The Paris Review, poetry ed. Richard Howard. 541 East 72nd Street, New York, N.Y. 10021.

Partisan Review, poetry ed. Rosanna Warren. Boston University, 141 Bay State Road, Boston, Mass. 02215.

Pequod, ed. Mark Rudman. Department of English, Room 200, New York University, 19 University Place, New York, N.Y. 10003.

Ploughshares, poetry ed. David Daniel. Emerson College, 100 Beacon Street, Boston, Mass. 02116.

Poetry, ed. Joseph Parisi. 60 West Walton Street, Chicago, Ill. 60610.

Princeton University Library Chronicle, ed. Patricia H. Marks. Princeton University Library, One Washington Road, Princeton, N.J. 08544–2098.

Salmagundi, ed. Robert Boyers. Skidmore College, Saratoga Springs, N.Y. 12866.

Sewanee Theological Review, poetry ed. Wyatt Prunty. University of the South, Sewanee, Tenn. 37375.

The Southern Review, eds. James Olney and Dave Smith. 43 Allen Hall, Louisiana State University, Baton Rouge, La. 70803–5005.

Southwest Review, ed. Willard Spiegelman. Southern Methodist University, Dallas, Tex. 75275.

The Stud Duck, ed. Mitchell Sisskind. 5042 Wilshire Boulevard, #402, Los Angeles, Calif. 90036.

The Tampa Review, ed. Richard Mathews. University of Tampa, 401 W. Kennedy Blvd., Box 19F, Tampa, Florida 33606–1490.

Threepenny Review, ed. Wendy Lesser. P.O. Box 9131, Berkeley, Calif. 94709.

Tikkun, poetry ed. Marge Piercy. P.O. Box 1778, Cathedral Station, New York, N.Y. 10025.

TriQuarterly, ed. Reginald Gibbons. Northwestern University, 2020 Ridge Avenue, Evanston, Ill. 60208.

Urbanus, ed. Peter Drizhal. P.O. Box 192561, San Francisco, Calif. 94119.

Western Humanities Review, poetry ed. Richard Howard. 341 Orson Spenser Hall, University of Utah, Salt Lake City, Utah 84112.

Witness, ed. Peter Stine. Oakland Community College, Orchard Ridge Campus, 27055 Orchard Lake Road, Farmington Hills, Mich. 48334.

The Yale Review, ed. J. D. McClatchy. P.O. Box 1902A, Yale Station, New Haven, Conn. 06520.

ZYZZYVA, ed. Howard Junker. 41 Sutter, Suite 1400, San Francisco, Calif. 94104.

ACKNOWLEDGMENTS

The series editor wishes to thank his assistant, Maggie Nelson, as well as Glen Hartley and Lynn Chu of Writers' Representatives, Inc., and Hamilton Cain of Scribner.

Grateful acknowledgment is made to the publications from which the poems in this volume were chosen. Unless specifically noted otherwise, copyright of the poems is held by the individual poets.

Margaret Atwood: "Bored" appeared in *The Atlantic Monthly*. Reprinted by permission of the poet.

Sally Ball: "Nocturnal" appeared in *Southwest Review*. Reprinted by permission of the poet.

Catherine Bowman: "Mr. X" appeared in *Chelsea* #55 and in *1-800-HOT-RIBS* (Peregrine Smith). Copyright © 1993 by Catherine Bowman. Reprinted by permission of Gibbs Smith, Publisher.

Stephanie Brown: "Schadenfreude" appeared in *American Poetry Review*. Reprinted by permission of the poet.

Lewis Buzbee: "Sunday, Tarzan in His Hammock" appeared in *ZYZZYVA* and was reprinted in *Harper's*. Reprinted by permission of the poet.

Cathleen Calbert: "The Woman Who Loved Things" appeared in *Harvard Review*. Reprinted by permission of the poet.

Rafael Campo: "The Battle Hymn of the Republic" appeared in *Ploughshares*. Reprinted by permission of the poet.

William Carpenter: "Girl Writing a Letter" appeared in *The Iowa Review*. Reprinted by permission of the poet.

Nicholas Christopher: "Terminus" appeared in *The Paris Review*. Reprinted by permission of the poet.

Jane Cooper: "The Infusion Room" from *Green Notebook, Winter Road* by Jane Cooper. Copyright © 1994 by Jane Cooper. Reprinted by permission of the poet and Tilbury House, Publishers. The poem originally appeared in *American Poetry Review*.

James Cummins: "Sestina" appeared in *The Paris Review*. Reprinted by permission of the poet.

Olena Kalytiak Davis: "Thirty Years Rising" appeared in *Michigan Quarterly Review*. Reprinted by permission of the poet.

Lynn Emanuel: "Film Noir: Train Trip Out of Metropolis" appeared in *The Antioch Review*. Reprinted by permission of the poet.

Elaine Equi: "Sometimes I Get Distracted" appeared in *New American Writing*. Reprinted by permission of the poet.

Irving Feldman: "Terminal Laughs" from *The Life and Letters* by Irving Feldman (University of Chicago Press). Copyright © 1994 by Irving Feld-

CUMULATIVE SERIES INDEX

The following are the annual listings in alphabetical order of poets and poems reprinted in the first seven editions of *The Best American Poetry*

1988
Edited and Introduced by John Ashbery

1989
Edited and Introduced by Donald Hall

1990
Edited and Introduced by Jorie Graham

1991
Edited and Introduced by Mark Strand

1992
Edited and Introduced by Charles Simic

1993
Edited and Introduced by Louise Glück

1994
Edited and Introduced by A. R. Ammons

ALSO AVAILABLE FROM
THE BEST AMERICAN POETRY SERIES

0-02-044182-7   THE BEST AMERICAN POETRY 1989
Edited by Donald Hall

0-02-032785-4   THE BEST AMERICAN POETRY 1990
Edited by Jorie Graham

0-02-069844-5   THE BEST AMERICAN POETRY 1991
Edited by Mark Strand

0-02-069845-3   THE BEST AMERICAN POETRY 1992
Edited by Charles Simic

0-02-069846-1   THE BEST AMERICAN POETRY 1993
Edited by Louise Glück

0-671-89948-1   THE BEST AMERICAN POETRY 1994
Edited by A. R. Ammons